T0246967

THE
PASSION
TRANSLATION

THE PASSIONATE LIFE BIBLE STUDY SERIES

12-LESSON STUDY GUIDE

THE BOOK OF
LUKE

TO THE LOVERS OF GOD

BroadStreet
PUBLISHING

BroadStreet Publishing® Group, LLC
Savage, Minnesota, USA
BroadStreetPublishing.com

TPT: The Gospel of Luke: 12-Lesson Bible Study Guide
Copyright © 2024 BroadStreet Publishing Group

9781424567607 (softcover)
9781424567614 (e-book)

Stock or custom editions of BroadStreet Publishing titles may be purchased in bulk for educational, business, ministry, fundraising, or sales promotional use. For information, please email info@broadstreetpublishing.com.

General editor: Dr. Brian Simmons
Managing editor: William D. Watkins
Writer: William D. Watkins

Design and typesetting Garborg Design Works| garborgdesign.com

Printed in China

24 25 26 27 28   5 4 3 2 1

Contents

From God's Heart to Yours

"God is love," says the apostle John, and "Everyone who loves is fathered by God and experiences an intimate knowledge of him" (1 John 4:7). The life of a Christ-follower is, at its core, a life of love—God's love of us, our love of him, and our love of others and ourselves because of God's love for us.

And this divine love is reliable, trustworthy, unconditional, other-centered, majestic, forgiving, redemptive, patient, kind, and more precious than anything else we can ever receive or give. It characterizes each person of the Trinity—Father, Son, and Holy Spirit—and so is as limitless as they are. They love one another with this eternal love, and they reach beyond themselves to us, created in their image with this love.

How do we know such incredible truths? Through the primary source of all else we know about the one God—his Word, the Bible. Of course, God reveals who he is through other sources as well, such as the natural world, miracles, our inner life, our relationships (especially with him), those who minister on his behalf, and those who proclaim him to us and others. But the fullest and most comprehensive revelation we have of God and from him is what he has given us in the thirty-nine books of the Hebrew Scriptures (the Old Testament) and the twenty-seven books of the Christian Scriptures (the New Testament). Together, these sixty-six books present a compelling and telling portrait of God and his dealings with us.

It is these Scriptures that *The Passionate Life Bible Study Series* is all about. Through these study guides, we—the editors and writers of this series—seek to provide you with a unique and welcoming opportunity to delve more deeply into God's precious Word, encountering there his loving heart for you and all the others he loves. God wants you to know him more deeply, to love him more devoutly, and to share his heart with others more frequently and freely. To accomplish this, we have based this study guide series on The Passion Translation of the Bible, which strives to "reintroduce the passion and fire of the Bible to the English reader. It doesn't merely convey the literal meaning of words. It expresses God's passion for people and his world by translating the original, life-changing message of God's Word for modern readers." It has been created to "kindle in you a burning desire to know the heart of God, while impacting the church for years to come."[1]

In each study guide, you will find an introduction to the Bible book it covers. There you will gain information about that Bible book's authorship, date of composition, first recipients, setting, purpose, central message, and key themes. Each lesson following the introduction will take a portion of that Bible book and walk you through it so you will learn its content better while experiencing and applying God's heart for your own life and encountering ways you can share his heart with others. Along the way, you will come across a number of features we have created that provide opportunities for more life application and growth in biblical understanding.

 Experience God's Heart

This feature focuses questions on personal application. It will help you live out God's Word and to bring the Bible into your world in fresh, exciting, and relevant ways.

 Share God's Heart

This feature will help you grow in your ability to share with other people what you learn and apply in a given lesson. It provides guidance on using the lesson to grow closer to others and to enrich your fellowship with others. It also points the way to enabling you to better listen to the stories of others so you can bridge the biblical story with their stories.

The Backstory

This feature provides ancient historical and cultural background that illuminates Bible passages and teachings. It deals with then-pertinent religious groups, communities, leaders, disputes, business trades, travel routes, customs, nations, political factions, ancient measurements and currency...in short, anything historical or cultural that will help you better understand what Scripture says and means.

 Word Wealth

This feature provides definitions for and other illuminating information about key terms, names, and concepts, and how different ancient languages have influenced the biblical text. It also provides insight into the different literary forms in the Bible, such as prophecy, poetry, narrative history, parables, and letters, and how knowing the form of a text can help you better interpret and apply it. Finally, this feature highlights the most significant passages in a Bible book. You may be encouraged to memorize these verses or keep them before you in some way so you can actively hide God's Word in your heart.

 Digging Deeper

This feature explains the theological significance of a text or the controversial issues that arise and mentions resources you can use to help you arrive at your own conclusions. Another way to dig deeper into the Word is by looking into the life of a biblical character or another person from church history, showing how that man or woman incarnated a biblical truth or passage. For instance, Jonathan Edwards was well known for his missions work among native American Indians and for his intellectual prowess in articulating the Christian faith, Florence Nightingale for the reforms she brought about in healthcare, Irenaeus for his fight against heresy, Billy Graham for his work in evangelism, Moses for the strength God gave him to lead the Hebrews and receive and communicate the law, and Deborah for her work as a judge in Israel. This feature introduces to you figures from the past who model what it looks like to experience God's heart and share his heart with others.

The Extra Mile

While The Passion Translation's notes are extensive, sometimes students of Scripture like to explore more on their own. In this feature, we provide you with opportunities to glean more information from a Bible dictionary, a Bible encyclopedia, a reliable Bible online tool, another ancient text, and the like. Here you will learn how you can go the extra mile on a Bible lesson. And not just in study either. Reflection, prayer, discussion, and applying a passage in new ways provide even more opportunities to go the extra mile. Here you will find questions to answer and applications to make that will require more time and energy from you—if and when you have them to give.

As you can see above, each of these features has a corresponding icon so you can quickly and easily identify them.

You will find other helps and guidance through the lessons of these study guides, including thoughtful questions, application suggestions, and spaces for you to record your own reflections, answers, and action steps. Of course, you can also write in your own journal, notebook, computer document, or other resource, but we have provided you with space for your convenience.

Also, each lesson will direct you toward the introductory material and numerous notes provided in The Passion Translation. There each Bible book contains a number of aids supplied to help you better grasp God's words and his incredible love, power, knowledge, plans, and so much more. We want you to get the most out of your Bible study, especially using it to draw you closer to the One who loves you most.

Finally, at the end of each lesson you'll find a section called "Talking It Out." This contains questions and exercises for application that you can share, answer, and apply with your spouse, a friend, a coworker, a Bible study group, or any other individuals or groups who would like to walk with you through this material. As Christians, we gather together to serve, study, worship, sing, evangelize, and a host of other activities. We grow together, not just on our own. This section will give you ample opportunities to engage others with some of the content of each lesson so you can work it out in community.

We offer all of this to support you in becoming an even more faithful and loving disciple of Jesus Christ. A disciple in the ancient world was a student of her teacher, a follower of his master. Students study, and followers follow. Jesus' disciples are to sit at his feet and listen and learn and then do what he tells them and shows them to do. We have created *The Passionate Life Bible Study Series* to help you do what a disciple of Jesus is called to do.

So go.

Read God's words.

Hear what he has to say in them and through them.

Meditate on them.

Hide them in your heart.

Display their truths in your life.

Share their truths with others.

Let them ignite Jesus' passion and light in all you say and do.

Use them to help you fulfill what Jesus called his disciples to do: "Now wherever you go, make disciples of all nations, baptizing them in the name of the Father, the Son, and the Holy Spirit. And teach them to faithfully follow all that I have commanded you. And never forget that I am with you every day, even to the completion of this age" (Matthew 28:19–20).

And through all of this, let Jesus' love nourish your heart and allow that love to overflow into your relationships with others (John 15:9–13). For it was for love that Jesus came, served, died, rose from the dead, and ascended into heaven. This love he gives us. And this love he wants us to pass along to others.

Why I Love the Gospel of Luke

Imagine the joy of telling the world about Jesus Christ. Many of us are faithful to share our faith with family, friends, and coworkers, but Luke gets to share his firsthand account of Jesus Christ with the *whole world*.

I'm looking forward to meeting Dr. Luke one day. He wrote over a quarter of the New Testament with his Gospel and the book of Acts. What a brilliant author and disciple of our Lord Jesus! I read his account with a hungry heart, for I know he performed an "autopsy" with the facts of the life and ministry of our Lord Jesus.[2] That's why I love Luke's account; we can trust it.

Also, I love how Luke records Jesus' interactions with both men and women. As stated in our introduction to Luke:

> Luke writes about Jesus' ministry to
> women twenty-four times. This was
> somewhat controversial in the culture of
> his day. In fact, Luke uses an alternating
> narrative of one story about a man and the
> next story about a woman. Luke begins
> with the story of Zechariah, then moves to
> Mary. A focus on Simeon, then on Anna.
> The Roman centurion, then the widow of
> Nain. The good Samaritan, then Mary and
> Martha. This pattern continues throughout
> his Gospel.[3]

I think Luke, more than any other Gospel writer, portrays the humanity of our Lord Jesus. Jesus is a wonderful man who gets hungry and sleepy and who reaches out with such tender compassion. He is not afraid to touch a leper, kneel before a child, restore the health of a suffering woman, and forgive his sometimes way-ward followers. There is a human touch to the writings of Luke that has always moved my soul to want to know Jesus better.

Do you like prayer? Then you will love Luke's stirring book that gives us glimpses into the private prayer life of our Master while presenting challenging truths to inspire our hearts to higher realms of prayer. I love the emphasis on prayer I find in this anointed Gospel.

Front and center in all of Luke's chapters is our Lord Jesus Christ. We find a lengthy introduction to his birth and baptism, with loads of loving glimpses into the miracles and teachings that have transformed our lives. I think Luke may have been the first "Jesus freak" because of all the focus he places on the Son of Man, our glorious King. I love the Jesus-centeredness of Luke.

And I can't leave out one more reason why Luke is beloved to my heart. It is the one he writes it for: Theophilus. For centuries, scholars have dug through ancient manuscripts looking for this man named Theophilus, but he remains an invisible, unknown entity. Who was he? Was he a nobleman? Perhaps an aristocrat of his day? Luke describes him as "excellent" or "honorable." But the Greek word Luke uses to describe him could also be translated as "mighty." I wonder who this "mighty Theophilus" could be. And why could historians and Bible scholars never track him down in history?

One day, it dawned on me. This was not a person but a group of people. The word *Theophilus* might not even be a name but a description. It means "lover (friend) of God." I believe Luke wrote his Gospel for every "mighty (excellent) lover of God." That's *you*. Luke's Gospel was written for you. And that's why I love the book of Luke.

I know you're going to enjoy this study guide. Make it your own personal journey into the heart of Jesus Christ. Be sure to take some friends along with you on your trip through this book of God's Word.

Brian Simmons
General Editor

Luke and His Gospel: Getting Started

(Luke 1:1–4)

History and story—these are the basic hallmarks of the Gospel of Luke. The writer gives us history, what really happened in the past, but he tells it as a story—in fact, as the story of stories, the story that matters more than all others. It's the historical story of Jesus, and like all good stories, it includes a cast of characters, all of whom are just as real as Jesus: for example, Mary and Joseph, Elizabeth and Zechariah, King Herod, a prophet named John, Jesus' disciples, and religious leaders such as the Pharisees and Sadducees. Luke tells about good angels and demons, healings and parables, discussions and refutations, prophetic pronouncements, betrayals, trials, and executions. And the writer ends the story with a resurrection and an ascension, events that open to the rest of the story—the other part of the story that the writer tells in his follow-up book, the Acts of the Apostles. Throughout his Gospel, however, the central figure is the man Jesus, who, the writer maintains, is God's Son in the flesh. And that's the most remarkable, life-changing event in human history. Truly the story of all stories, the historical fact of all facts.

The Writer's Identity

The Gospel of Luke is the third of four Gospels, the others being Matthew, Mark, and John.

The earliest testimonies we have unanimously name Luke as the writer of the third Gospel book. The Gospel itself doesn't mention who its writer is, but early church leaders, such as Irenaeus (late second century), Clement of Alexandria (ca. 155–220), Origen (ca. 185–254), and Tertullian (ca. 160/70–215/20), specify that the author is Luke and that he also wrote the Acts of the Apostles. Even the heretic Marcion (ca. 135) named Luke as the writer of the third Gospel. Following such testimony, the church's tradition never wavered that Luke was the author of the third Gospel and that he was also the one who wrote Acts.

So what do we know about Luke the man?

As the author of Acts, he humbly mentions a time when he was traveling with the apostle Paul. Luke doesn't name himself, but the language changes from talking as a historian about Paul and his travels by using the third person voice ("they") to talking as a participant, a fellow traveler, using the second person voice "we" (Acts 16:10–17; 20:5–15; 21:1–18; 27:1–28:16). And Paul verifies Luke's companionship in his travels as well as mentioning Luke's medical vocation (Colossians 4:14; Philemon 24; 2 Timothy 4:11). As a physician and one of Paul's occasional traveling companions, Luke would have cared for the apostle's health needs. One scholar states that Luke was "Paul's medical adviser, and doubtless prolonged his life and rescued him from many a serious illness."[4]

- *Discover more about Dr. Luke by reading the opening paragraph of the section titled "Author and Audience" in The Passion Translation's introduction to the Gospel of Luke. Summarize what you find there about this early Christian.*

We don't know much about the man Luke. We do, however, know quite a bit about the writing he produced. He left us with the Gospel that bears his name and the follow-up book of Acts. Bible scholar Joseph Fitzmeyer wrote: "[Luke] was a perceptive, sensitive writer with a knack for telling a story and depicting a scene, and his *Gospel* has been described as 'the most beautiful book' ever written. His two books constitute the earliest history of the Christian church."[5]

Luke's vocabulary is extensive. Although he shares a good deal of his subject matter with Mark and Matthew, he "uses 266 words (other than proper names) which are not found elsewhere in the New Testament."[6] Another New Testament scholar points out that "Luke was a Greek who had the 'native instinct' not only to write well but to vary his style scene by scene...His writings are generally held to be superb in style and structure."[7]

So while we have little information about the human author, his writings tell us that he was a first-rate wordsmith and story-teller, and his attention to detail and historical accuracy tell us that he was a master historian. In fact, scholar William Ramsay, who went into his studies of Luke assuming that the writer was not a good historian, came to the conclusion that "Luke's history is unsurpassed in respect of its trustworthiness." He also said about Luke: "No writer is correct by mere chance, or accurate sporadically. He is accurate by virtue of a certain habit of mind," and this accuracy is "produced by his moral and intellectual character."[8] Luke shows through his writings that, intellectually, he was astute, and morally, he was a faithful member of the Way—a name that became attached to the Christian movement very early in its history.

- *What about the man Luke do you identify with?*

- *Luke was not an eyewitness of the events he records in his Gospel (Luke 1:1–4). This made him a second-generation Christian writing about the believers in Jesus who came first. What advantages, if any, do you think this gave him in the writing of his book?*

Luke's Audience, Purpose, and Date

Luke opens his Gospel unlike any of the other three Gospels in the New Testament.

- *Read Luke 1:1–4 and study note 'a' in TPT, then answer the following questions:*

     Whom did Luke address as the first recipient(s) of his Gospel?

     Did Luke know of other biographies of Jesus? Support your answer.

     Why did Luke choose to write his account of Jesus' life?

On what resources did he base his Gospel? Why do such resources matter in the writing of history, especially the history of a person's life?

- *Now compare Luke's opening verses with those of the other three Gospels. How does his opener differ from that of Matthew's, Mark's, and John's?*

  Matthew 1:1–17

  Mark 1:1

  John 1:1–5

In TPT, the phrase "mighty lover of God" gets at the heart of the Greek word *Theophilus*, the original recipient of Luke's Gospel (Luke 1:1). Much speculation has developed over the identity of Theophilus, for he is mentioned just twice in the New Testament (the other place is in Acts 1:1), and in both instances, Luke provides little information about him. All we know for certain is his name and what it means. This has led some scholars to wonder whether there ever was an individual named Theophilus. Perhaps Luke just meant to write his Gospel to anyone who identified as a lover or friend of God, especially those "non-Jewish lovers of God who may have felt out of place in the originally Jewish" side of the Christian movement.[9]

Whoever the original audience was, Luke strives to give them verified information about Jesus in the form of "an orderly account of what Jesus accomplished and fulfilled among us." Luke refers to his Gospel as an "accurate compilation of my own meticulous investigation based on numerous eyewitness interviews." His goal is to reassure his readers that what they had been taught about Jesus was true and trustworthy (Luke 1:1–4; cf. Acts 1:1).

- *Are you at a point in your life when you could use some reassurances about what you have learned about Jesus and his teachings? This Bible study on Luke's Gospel could help meet this need. Take some time to ask God to use this study to accomplish that for you and to meet other needs that arise as a result of learning and applying Luke's Gospel.*

Determining the time when Luke wrote his Gospel is based largely on Acts and what that book does and does not record. The opening words of Luke and Acts imply an order, with Luke as the first book and Acts the second one.

- *Review Luke 1:1–4 and Acts 1:1. What do you find there that would indicate that Acts was written after Luke and not before it?*

Also, the book of Acts does not mention several events that had a major impact on the early church—events that Luke would likely have mentioned if he had not yet concluded writing Acts. These omitted events include the following:

- In the spring of AD 62, the Jewish ruling body, the Sanhedrin, put to death James, the Lord's brother, without securing the permission of Roman authorities.
- In 64, the Roman emperor Nero brought cruel and

controversial atrocities upon Christians in the city of Rome and its surrounding districts.

- Between 64 and 68, the apostles Peter and Paul were executed in Rome under the emperor Nero's reign.

- The Zealots, a Jewish party who worked to purge Israel of its Roman overlords, led an armed revolt against the Romans from 66 to 73. The church historian Eusebius (ca. 265–339) records a tradition that, before the war against Rome began, "believers had been warned through a prophetic utterance to flee from Jerusalem to the city of Pella in Perea...Perhaps some Jerusalem believers remembered the words of Jesus (Matt. 24:15–16 [parallels Mark 13:14; Luke 21:20–21]): 'So when you see standing in the holy place "the abomination that causes desolation," spoken of through the prophet Daniel—let the reader understand—then let those who are in Judea flee to the mountains.'"[10] And this Christians did—in droves!

- In the year 70, the Romans besieged Jerusalem and ultimately looted and destroyed the city and its temple. Hundreds of thousands of civilians and rebels died in the process, including children.[11]

That Luke fails to mention any of these events indicates that he had completed writing his Gospel and Acts before they took place. This is especially telling for the destruction of Jerusalem and its temple in 70. Since Jesus had predicted their destruction (Matthew 24:1–2, 15–18; Mark 13:1–2; Luke 21:20–24), it would be incredibly odd, if not astonishing, for Luke to omit them. After all, they further confirmed Jesus' accuracy as a prophet.

When scholars put these facts (and others) together, they put the writing of Luke's Gospel anywhere between the years 57 and 61.[12]

Major Characteristics

In telling Jesus' story, Luke emphasizes certain aspects of it that especially stand out.

A Fuller History

Luke's Gospel tells more of Jesus' story than any of the other three Gospels. In fact, his Gospel is the longest book in the New Testament. Luke gives us a fuller account of Jesus' birth and childhood and informs us about John the Baptist's conception and birth. Luke presents many parables of Jesus not found in the other Gospels, such as the parables of the good Samaritan, the wealthy fool, the prodigal son, and the rich man and Lazarus. Luke also provides evidence of Jesus' post-resurrection activity not found in the other Gospels, and he's the only Gospel writer to describe Jesus' ascension.

- *Each of the four Gospels presents the story of Jesus, and they do this from different angles, with different emphases, and with different purposes. In TPT, read the "About" and "Purpose" sections in the introduction to each Gospel. Summarize key features of each Gospel described there.*

Matthew's Gospel –

Mark's Gospel –

Luke's Gospel –

John's Gospel –

- *Now consider how the combination of these key features helps us fill out the larger reality of Jesus. What might we have missed if we had just one of these Gospels or perhaps just two or even three of them?*

The Gospel's Universality

Luke presents the gospel as good news for all and available to all no matter their social or economic status, their gender or nationality, their Jewishness or non-Jewishness, their age maturity, or anything else that differentiates people. As one Bible commentator said:

> Luke emphasized the universal message of the gospel more than the other Gospel writers. He often wrote about sinners, the poor, and outcasts from Jewish society. He also referred many times to Gentiles who shared in the blessings of the Messiah. Samaritans were presented as coming to faith in the Messiah. And Luke wrote frequently of women and children and their faith.[13]

- *Do you see that the gospel (the good news) of Jesus is for everyone? Why or why not?*

Women and the Poor

Brian Simmons, in his introduction to the Gospel of Luke, summarizes well the book's emphasis on women and the poor:

> In Luke's Gospel they [women] provide
> examples of deep piety and devotion.
> They are both of humble means and
> wealthy. At every turn women are part of
> Jesus' ministry: Elizabeth, Anna, and of
> course Mary play important roles in his
> infancy; women are healed, comforted,
> and forgiven in Galilee; on the way to
> Jerusalem, we meet Mary and Martha;
> and during Christ's most desperate hours,
> women weep at his feet, stand with him
> faithfully; finally, they receive the first
> revelation of Jesus' resurrection. Then
> there are the poor. Throughout Luke, the
> poor receive special attention too, showing
> that God deliberately reaches out to those
> whom society casts away. He makes clear
> the good news of Jesus and his love is for
> people like them, which means the gospel
> truly is for everybody![14]

• *Do you harbor any biases against males or females? If so, what are they? If you do, have any of your biases influenced with whom you share the good news about Jesus? Why or why not?*

- *How about when it comes to a person's economic status? Do you believe that the poor should or should not hear the good news about Jesus? Why or why not?*

The Significance of Prayer

Prayer in action and teaching about prayer are important aspects of Luke's presentation, and Jesus is at the heart of both. Jesus prays on numerous occasions: at his baptism (Luke 3:21), after ministering to the crowds (5:16), before choosing his closest twelve disciples (6:12), before Peter's declaration of Jesus' identity and Jesus' prediction of his own death and resurrection (9:18), at the time of his transfiguration (vv. 28–29), on the return of the seventy disciples from ministry (10:21), before teaching the disciples to pray (11:1), in Gethsemane (22:39–46), and twice while hanging on the cross (23:34, 46). New Testament scholar Robert Gundry observes that "almost all these references to Jesus' prayers are distinctive to Luke." Moreover, "Only Luke records two parables of Jesus about prayer (11:5–13; 18:1–8) and informs us that Jesus had prayed especially for Peter (22:31–32)."[15]

- *What is your prayer life like? Describe it.*

- *What about prayer do you hope Jesus will address in Luke's Gospel?*

The Presence and Work of the Spirit

The Holy Spirit is prominent in Luke's Gospel from the beginning to the end. While Luke presents Jesus' story first and foremost, he acknowledges the centrality of the Spirit in this story. This Gospel references the Spirit almost twenty times. The Spirit is "the driving force in the picture Luke paints of God's coming salvation. He is the architect, the maestro guiding and energizing the events that transpire throughout the life of Jesus. We find him present from the very beginning with his conception and birth on to Christ's baptism in the Spirit and through to his powerful miracle ministry."[16] The Spirit also fills John the Baptist (1:15) and Elizabeth, his mother (v. 41). The Spirit is also upon Simeon who, through the Spirit, praises God and prophesies concerning Jesus as the Messiah (2:25–35). During his ministry, Jesus tells his disciples that God the Father would give the Holy Spirit to those who asked (11:13). And after his resurrection, Jesus promises the disciples that they will soon be "clothed with the mighty power of heaven" (24:49)—that is, with the Holy Spirit. The Gospel of Luke is the story of Jesus intertwined with the presence and power of the Spirit of God.

- *Later in this study, we'll dig deeper into the Spirit's relationship with Jesus and what it reveals about the kind of relationship we can have with the Spirit. For now, we suggest that you commit to asking the Lord to fill you with his Spirit as you pursue this study of Luke's Gospel. Ask the Spirit to illumine your mind and awaken your heart to the truths embedded in Luke and to empower you to grow deeper in Christ and live more like him each day.*

Praise and Joy

Yet another distinctive emphasis of this Gospel is the praise and joy found throughout it. Bible scholar Leon Morris brings this out clearly:

> Luke's is a singing Gospel. Here are some of the great hymns of the Christian faith: the glory song of the angels (2:14), the *Magnificat*, the *Benedictus* and the *Nunc Dimittis* (1:46ff., 68ff.; 2:29ff.). Quite often people who receive benefits praise God or glorify God or the like (2:20; 5:25f.; 7:16; 13:13; 17:15; 18:43). The verb 'rejoice' occurs more often in Luke than in any other New Testament book and the noun 'joy' also occurs often (e.g., 1:14, 44, 47; 10:21). There is laughter in this Gospel (6:21) and merry-making (15:23, 32). There is joy in Zacchaeus' reception of Jesus (19:6). There is joy on earth over the finding of the lost sheep and the lost coin and there is joy in heaven over the finding of lost sinners (15:6f., 9f.) And this Gospel finishes, as it had begun, with rejoicing (24:52; cf. 1:14).[17]

- *Sometimes it can be quite difficult to praise God and express joy in our fallen, broken world. It wasn't easy to do so in Jesus' day either—a fact that will become ever clearer as we get further along in our study of Luke. Still, we can always find a reason to rejoice, to be glad in the Lord. Take some time right now to reflect on your life and your relationship with God, focusing especially on what you can be grateful for. Write your list here, then offer your thanksgiving to the Lord for what he has done for you and through you.*

 EXPERIENCE GOD'S HEART

- *Choose anything you learned in this introduction to Luke's Gospel that especially resonated with you and summarize it below.*

- *Why do you think this has significance for you?*

- *Now pray that God will deepen this matter in your life so you come to understand it even better than you do now and that he will use it to draw you ever closer to him and his ways.*

SHARE GOD'S HEART

- *Whom do you know who needs to know more about Jesus or perhaps be introduced to him for the first time? List anywhere from two to six people and pray that God will provide opportunities for them to hear the gospel of Jesus. Remain open to the possibility that God will provide the way for you to be an answer to this prayer.*

- *Post a list of these individuals where you will see it often. Pray for them as often as you can. Then find ways to check in on them from time to time to see how they are doing. As we'll see, Jesus got involved in the lives of others, which is one reason why he was so effective at ministering to them in the ways they needed most.*

Talking It Out

Since Christians grow in community, not just in solitude, every "Talking It Out" section contains questions you may want to discuss with another person or in a group. Here are the exercises for this lesson.

1. Luke was a behind-the-camera storyteller in his Gospel. He kept the story's focus on Jesus even when the narrative started before Jesus' conception and birth, and he kept himself out of the storyline. What are some advantages to telling the gospel story this way? What may be some disadvantages?

2. Dr. Luke relied on eyewitness testimony for what he records in his Gospel. How does eyewitness testimony compare to hearsay? What are some checks that eyewitnesses can bring to secondhand and even thirdhand testimony?

3. Share with one another the story of how you came to know Jesus. Then spend some time celebrating together the gift of the gospel and how it has changed your life.

LESSON 1

The Prophet and the Savior

(Luke 1:5–2:40)

All children are a blessing from the Lord (Psalm 127:3), but not all parents are ready for them. Luke introduces us to two couples: Elizabeth and Zechariah and Mary and Joseph. Elizabeth and Zechariah were an older couple and childless while Mary and Joseph were just beginning their marital journey and, appropriately, were childless. Neither couple was prepared for children but for different reasons. Yet God had children in mind for both couples, and the entrance of these children into the world would mark the start of lives that would forever shape world history.

The Historical Setting

Like a good historian, Dr. Luke gives us the historical backdrop for the events he's about to describe.

- *Who was the king at the time, and what was the primary region of his kingdom (Luke 1:5)?*

- *In TPT, turn to the maps section and find the map titled "The Holy Land in the Time of Jesus." Notice the regions designated as the "Kingdom of Herod the Great." Along with Judea, what other regions were under his control?*

 # THE BACKSTORY

During this time in history, all the land of Israel was under the authority of Rome. The Roman Empire was massive, covering about 2.5 million miles and, at its height, had a population of about one hundred million. The central capital was the city of Rome, and the territory under Rome's sway when Caesar Augustus was emperor (30 BC–AD 14) went as far west as Spain and Gaul and east to what we know today as Iraq. Its southern border was northern Africa and Egypt, and its northern border was the Danube River. Much of Europe and the entire Mediterranean world were Roman.

Herod first came to political power when his father, Antipater II, appointed him as the governor of Galilee in 47 BC. Herod was just twenty-five years old. The head of the Roman Republic at the time was Julius Caesar (47–44 BC). Caesar became the Republic's first dictator, an event that marked the end of the Roman Republic and the beginning of the Roman Empire. Soon after Caesar was assassinated in 44 in a failed attempt to restore the Republic, civil war erupted. Marc Antony, who had been Julius Caesar's deputy, still wielded authority, and he appointed Herod and his brother Phasael as tetrarchs (rulers) of Judea in 41. Herod's political power was growing.

In 40, the Parthians attacked and captured Jerusalem and set up a man named Antigonus as ruler. Antigonus was part of the long line of Hasmoneans who came to power in Palestine around 140 BC. Under the Parthians, Phasael was captured and put in chains, and Herod took his family and fled to Masada and then to Petra. Phasael died of poisoning or suicide (the historical record is unclear), and Herod then went to Rome where Antony persuaded the Roman senate to make Herod a king but still under Rome's power and authority. Nevertheless, Herod's new royal rights did not become fully effective until he "returned to Palestine, recaptured Galilee and finally captured Jerusalem in the summer of 37 B.C."[18] He then beheaded Antigonus and forever ended the rule of the Hasmonean Dynasty.

Herod then reestablished his rule over Galilee and added to it Judea. Later, around 30 BC, Octavius (the man who would become known as Caesar Augustus) extended Herod's authority to "Gadara, Hippos, Samaria, Gaza, Anthedon, Joppa, and Strato's Tower (which later became Caesarea)."[19] Herod ruled all this territory as king until 4 BC. During that time, he became a close friend to Augustus and established policies that greatly increased trade and commerce for the people he governed. He also increased the people's taxes and launched into and completed multiple building projects, which included amphitheaters, palaces, fortresses, cities, aqueducts, and what became his most notable achievement—the new temple in Jerusalem. Temple construction began around 20 BC and finished in AD 63, long after Herod had died. "The rabbis said, 'Whoever…has not seen the Temple of Herod has never seen a beautiful building.'"[20]

Herod could be generous. During years of famine, for example, he didn't collect taxes. On one occasion, "he even sold his dinnerware to buy food for the populace…He was so highly respected by Rome that he would actually go down in history as 'Herod the Great.'"[21]

However, many of his subjects disliked him. Herod was only half-Jew ethnically; he advanced Greco-Roman culture, education, and religion; his taxes were often a heavy burden for the people to carry; and he had ten wives, each wanting their sons to succeed in Herod's place.

> Soon he was hated as a tyrant, even by
> members of his own family. A maddening

maze of intrigues infested the palace, and Herod began suspecting everyone, tormented, as he was, by fears of assassination. In his advancing paranoia, he was continually writing to Rome for permission to execute one or two of his sons for treason. Finally, even his patron and friend Augustus had to admit, "I'd rather be Herod's pig than his son." It was not only a play on the similar-sounding Greek words for *son* and *pig*, but a wry reference to the fact that pork, at least, was not consumed by Jews.[22]

Herod, Luke says, was the king over the land in which two history-changing births would soon occur. And one of these newborns would be heralded by many as the King over all kings.

A Priestly Elderly Couple

Luke introduces us to a Jewish couple, Elizabeth and Zechariah.

• *What details does Luke provide about Zechariah (Luke 1:5–7)?*

• *What does he tell us about his wife, Elizabeth (vv. 5–7)?*

This was a priestly family, with Zechariah a priest in the order of Aaron, of which Abijah was a part, and Elizabeth the daughter of a priest. Leon Morris gives us some useful background information about this:

> There were many priests, but only one
> temple. So they served on a roster (1 Chr.
> 24:1–6). The priests were divided into
> twenty-four divisions of which that of *Abijah*
> was the eighth (1 Chr. 24:10)…Each division
> was on duty twice a year, for a week on
> each occasion. Zechariah was married to
> *Elizabeth*, a priest's daughter. A priest was
> required to marry an Israelite virgin (Lev.
> 21:14), but not necessarily one of a priestly
> family. To have a wife of priestly stock was
> a special blessing for a priest.[23]

What this couple had long lacked was a child—a situation that was about to be remedied.

- *Read Luke 1:8–10 and study note 'c.' What was Zechariah chosen to do? What was the significance to him?*

- *Who (what) appeared to Zechariah (vv. 11, 19), and what was this being's relationship to God?*

- *What was Zechariah's response to this being's appearance (v. 12)? Why do you suppose the priest reacted this way?*

- *What did this being say to Zechariah about the child to come, including what his ministry would be (vv. 13–17)?*

- *What role would the Holy Spirit play in this new person's life, and when would that role begin (v. 15)?*

- *How did Zechariah respond to such incredible news (v. 18)?*

- *What judgment did the angel pronounce on Zechariah, which would also serve as a sign of affirmation that what the angel said would undoubtedly occur (vv. 19–20)?*

- *What happened after Zechariah emerged from the temple (vv. 21–24)?*

- *Did Elizabeth become pregnant? How did she respond to her new condition (v. 25)?*

A Poor Young Couple

Now Luke turns to another Jewish couple, Mary and Joseph. They are not yet married but engaged to be so—an arrangement in ancient Judaism that was so significant and serious that to end it required a divorce (vv. 26–27; see also Matthew 1:18–19, including study notes 'g' and 'h'). The same angel who appeared to Zechariah came this time to the woman, Mary, and not to the man in her life. Mary was in Nazareth, the village where she lived, and her husband-to-be was a "descendant of King David"—but certainly not a member of royalty with any wealth or political power. Instead, it was Joseph's *ancestry* that went back to the great King David. Why did that matter? The angel would tell them.

- *When does the angel Gabriel appear to Mary (Luke 1:26–27)?*

- *Luke describes Mary as "an unmarried girl" (vv. 26–27). Read study note 'g' and summarize what you find there about this wording and what else Luke says about Mary's circumstances at this time.*

- *After Gabriel first addressed Mary, how did she respond (vv. 28–29)?*

- *What was Gabriel's good news for Mary (vv. 30–33)?*

- *Review verses 32–33. What did Gabriel say here that connected with Joseph's Davidic lineage? Compare this with 2 Samuel 7:12–17 and Psalm 89:19–29. What role would Jesus forever fulfill?*

- *What was Mary's response to Gabriel's announcement (Luke 1:34)?*

- *What was Gabriel's answer to Mary's question (vv. 35–37)?*

- *What would be the Spirit's role in Jesus' life, and when would it begin (v. 35)?*

- *With Gabriel's announcement complete, what was Mary's final response (v. 38)? Compare and contrast her response to the angel's news with how Zechariah reacted.*

The Mothers' Exchange

Soon after Mary's encounter with Gabriel, she went "to the hill country of Judea, to the village where Zechariah and Elizabeth lived" (v. 39). When Mary entered their home, Elizabeth, who was her relative (perhaps her aunt), experienced dramatic and unusual movement within her.

- *What did Elizabeth experience within her womb (v. 41)?*

- *What did she experience from God's Spirit (vv. 41–42)?*

- *Empowered by the Spirit, what did Elizabeth proclaim (vv. 42–45)?*

Elizabeth's Spirit-inspired expression of wonder, honor, and joy led Mary, also Spirit-empowered, to break out in poetic song.

- *Read verses 46–55. Write down your impressions and emotions as you pore over Mary's outburst of joy and praise.*

- *In these verses, what did Mary express about herself?*

- *What did she ascribe to the "Mighty One" (v. 49)?*

- *Summarize what she exclaimed about the child still growing in her womb.*

Mary remained with Elizabeth perhaps through the rest of Elizabeth's pregnancy (v. 56; cf. vv. 26–27).

The Prophet's Birth

Just as Gabriel had said, Elizabeth gave birth to a son, an event met with great joy by all those who knew her and Zechariah (vv. 57–58). Then, on the eighth day after the boy's birth, Elizabeth and Zechariah followed the long-established Jewish custom of having their son circumcised (v. 59).

- *For the family and friends who had gathered for the circumcision ceremony, what did they expect Zechariah and Elizabeth would name the newborn? Why were they surprised when Elizabeth told them that their son's name would be different (vv. 59–61)?*

- *How did Zechariah back up his wife, and what was the response of those who heard this news (vv. 62–66)?*

- *Once again, the Spirit made his presence and power known through Zechariah. What did this priest prophesy about the yet unborn Jesus (vv. 68–75)?*

- *Summarize what Zechariah prophesied about his own newly born son (vv. 76–77).*

- *Finally, Zechariah closed out his prophetic utterance by proclaiming what God was about to do for his people. Notice the comparison he made between light and darkness (vv. 78–79). Now read John's use of the same imagery in the Gospel of John 1:4–9. Jot down the similarities you see between John's description of Jesus and Zechariah's description of God's then coming work.*

- *Luke summarizes John's life in Luke 1:80. What does Luke say that John did, and who empowered John to become the man he was and to live the way he did?*

The Messiah's Birth

With the forerunner John now born, it was time for the long-expected Messiah to break into daylight. The Hebrew prophets had said that the Messiah would be born in Bethlehem (Micah 5:2), but Mary and Joseph lived in Nazareth. The distance between these two small towns was about sixty-five miles, which, by foot, would have taken several days to travel.[24] So how would the prophecy be fulfilled? God would use a gentile Roman census to get this Jewish couple to the prophesied city.

The Political Context

Just as Luke had provided a historical marker for John's conception and birth (Luke 1:5), so he does for Jesus' birth (2:1–2).

- *Who was the ruler when Gabriel told Zechariah of John's conception and birth, and over what territory was his primary authority (1:5)?*

- *Who was the ruler over the entire Roman Empire, and what did he order that led Jesus' expected birthplace to change (2:1–2)?*

- *Who was Quirinius (vv. 1–2)?*

⊘ DIGGING DEEPER

A lot of ink has been spilled over the opening verses of Luke chapter 2. The issues concern the timing of the census, the governorship of Quirinius, and the birth year of Jesus. We have historical evidence outside of Scripture that Augustus had initiated at least three censuses before he died in AD 14: one in 28 BC, another in 8 BC, and the last in AD 14. Other censuses had occurred besides these, and many of these were of different regions within the empire but not conducted empire wide. So which census is Luke referring to?

Then there's the matter of Quirinius. We have firm evidence that he governed Syria briefly between AD 6 and 7, and during that time, he conducted a census that included Judea. The problem is that this census was too late to link to Jesus' birth year, for he had already been born (scholars typically date Jesus' birth between 7 and 4 BC). So do we have reason to believe that Quirinius may have been governor of Syria earlier and conducted a census then? If so, Quirinius overseeing a census would have had to occur while Herod the Great was still alive, in other words, prior to his death in the spring of 4 BC, for Jesus was born while Herod was still reigning in Palestine. Is there such evidence? Corey Piper, in his recent book *500 Year Journey: From Babylon to Bethlehem*, writes:

> There are some ancient inscriptions that have been found that have led some scholars to place Quirinius in the region when Herod was alive. However, these inscriptions do not mention Quirinius by name, and there is no reason to think that even if he were in the region of Syria in 7 BC that he had anything to do with the management of a census in Judea. There were already two very competent Romans in charge at that time—Saturninus and Voluminus. Did yet a third high-ranking

> Roman need to be there, especially to oversee a census?[25]

So what's the solution? Piper and others argue that it's found partly in the Greek grammar of Luke's statement in Luke 2:1–2. Instead of "Quirinius was the governor of Syria at that time," the Greek may be rendered as "This registration [census] was before Quirinius governed Syria," as David Garland translates it,[26] or "This was the first of the series of registrations which occurred before Quirinius took command of Syria," which is the way Piper translates it.[27] New Testament scholar Harold Hoehner also embraces this understanding in his book *Chronological Aspects of the Life of Christ*.[28]

So if the census that led Mary and Joseph to Bethlehem was *not* the one actually conducted under Quirinius, why mention Quirinius at all? Perhaps because the census Quirinius oversaw was seared into the minds and hearts of Luke's first readers unlike any other they had ever experienced. Quirinius's census in the early first century fomented an armed rebellion led by a Galilean Jew named Judas. This was the first census imposed on the Jews that the Romans conducted directly rather than indirectly through client rulers such as Herod the Great and the sons of his who ruled after him. Judas saw this Roman imposition as an "introduction to slavery," said the first-century Jewish historian Josephus, and he urged his fellow countrymen to fight against it and thereby retain their freedom. This marked the beginning of the Zealot movement that "burgeoned into a pattern of sedition and conflict and culminated in the revolt against Rome and Jerusalem's destruction" in AD 70.[29] Piper puts the significance of this initial Judas-led revolt this way: "What happened during this census was a significant moment in Jewish history—the equivalent of Japan's attack on Pearl Harbor in 1941 or the terrorist airplane attacks on US targets on September 11, 2001."[30]

In Acts 5, the Jewish religious leader Gamaliel refers to this census and revolt as part of his rationale for treating Peter and the other apostles with care. Gamaliel reminds the Sanhedrin, "In the days of the census, another man rose up, Judas the Galilean, who got people to follow him in a revolt. He too perished, and all those who followed him were scattered. So in this situation [with the apostles], you should just leave these men to themselves" (vv. 37–38). Notice that Gamaliel refers to "the census" and what Judas had done in response to it. He didn't need to say anything else for everyone hearing him to know which census he had in mind. It was similar for Luke and his first readers. When Luke mentioned Quirinius and the infamous census he had conducted, everyone knew what he was talking about.

In short, what Luke says is that Jesus was born under the reigns of Herod the Great and Caesar Augustus and *before* the census of Quirinius, the infamous census that led to armed resistance and the rise of the Zealot movement.

- *What are some major historical events that you might use*
  as markers for people to grasp when something important
  to you took place? Why are these events significant
  enough to use this way?

The Towns

Because of the demands of the Roman census, Mary and Joseph had to leave their home in Nazareth and travel to Bethlehem, where they would register for purposes of taxation and to record their loyalty to Rome (Luke 2:4–5). Nazareth was a small village in the hill country about fifteen miles from the Sea of Galilee. No main roads passed through it or near it. If you wanted to visit it, you had to go out of your way to get there. It was also an insignificant village.

Most everybody's homesite has at least one
claim to fame—a battle which was fought
there, a major accomplishment by some of
its citizens, a famous person who was born

there. Not Nazareth. Not a single reference to Nazareth can be found in any of the ancient non-Christian literature, in the Jewish Talmud, or even in the published works of Josephus, the Jewish historian who seemed to write about everybody and everything.[31]

- *What is your hometown like? Is it comparable to Nazareth, perhaps a bit better known, or even well-known, such as Chicago, London, or Paris?*

- *What was it like growing up where you lived? Was it a place where you wanted to stay or one you wanted to leave?*

Bethlehem, on the other hand, had a notable history and a famous family line linked to it. It had been "King David's ancient home" (vv. 4–5). It was also the setting for the story of Ruth (Ruth 1:1, 19), and the place where the prophet Samuel had anointed David king (1 Samuel 16:1–13). Micah had prophesied centuries before that the Messiah would come from Bethlehem (Micah 5:2). Bethlehem mattered. But not as a holy place. "Most folks associated Bethlehem with government and politics. Herod lived there. Tax collectors and census takers worked there. Not by the farthest stretch of the imagination could a trip to Bethlehem qualify as a spiritual pilgrimage."[32] The birth of Jesus would change all of this.

- *Consider the information provided in TPT study note 'e' for Luke 2:4–5. Summarize what you learn there about Bethlehem.*

- *Return to these passages in Luke—1:27, 32–33, 69; 2:4—and consider what they say about David and the Messiah. How might they relate to the unborn Jesus ending up in Bethlehem? Is there at least a partial fulfillment of prophecy occurring? Explain your answer.*

The Birth of All Births

- *Where did Mary give birth (2:6–7)? Check out study note 'g' and add below any relevant information it provides to your answer.*

- *Jesus' birth was accompanied by a heavenly announcement (vv. 8–14). Describe the scene and what happened in your own words.*

- *What did the shepherds do after the heavenly messengers left them (vv. 15–20)? And how did Mary respond to all of this (v. 19)?*

 # THE BACKSTORY

What Luke doesn't say—but his first readers would have known—is that Jesus' birth occurred in King Herod's backyard. Bethlehem was the site of Herod's beautiful home:

> Herod's majestic palace towered over all of the other buildings in Bethlehem—by far the most impressive structure in the region. Its size communicated authority and its grandiose beauty intimated the power of its owner and the significance of his decisions. For years, people had looked for God's Messiah to take the government upon His shoulders, implement a major shift in power, and elevate the nation of Israel to a new plateau of political sovereignty. Herod's palace seemed to be the only place in town worthy of the Messiah's entrance into history.[33]

And yet, the Messiah wasn't born in Herod's palace but in the shadow of that huge, gorgeous structure. He came into the world in the boarding room of one of Herod's subjects, a room that also housed animals, and there he slept in a "feeding trough" (v. 7). The King of kings and Lord of lords came humbly, as a servant, not as the royalty he was and is.

 EXPERIENCE GOD'S HEART

- *What is your position in life? Are you high up in your church, your family, or your career? Do others look up to you? If so, do you relish the attention and honor, or do you respond with humility? Explain your answer.*

- *Perhaps your position in life is much less noticed and respected. Maybe you are even taken for granted occasionally or often. That kind of treatment can be hurtful, especially when you feel others owe you more. Jesus was certainly due a much greater entrance into our world than he received. Yes, angels announced his birth, not to kings or emperors but to shepherds, and not in cities but out in a field away from any major population center. What does this reveal about God's heart? How might that relate to you and how you view your circumstances?*

Dedication and Recognition

Just as John's parents brought him before God for circumcision, so Jesus' parents did for their son. And Jesus received the name that the angel Gabriel said he should receive, just as John had received the name that Gabriel had announced to his parents (1:13, 31, 59–63; 2:21–24).

- *What prescribed sacrifice did Joseph and Mary bring with them for the circumcision and dedication of Jesus (vv. 23–24)? What did it signify about this Jewish couple (see study note 'd' for verse 24)?*

- *Who was Simeon, and what was the role that the Spirit played in his life (vv. 25–27)?*

- *What did Simeon prophesy over the baby Jesus and Mary (vv. 28–35)?*

- *Who was Anna, and what had she been doing before God for many years (vv. 36–37)?*

- *What did Anna do that confirmed Simeon's message about Jesus (v. 38)?*

❤ SHARE GOD'S HEART

Simeon and Anna had both committed themselves to God and so were prepared to encounter the Savior when Joseph and Mary brought him near. And they shared what they knew, not just with Jesus' parents but also with others, including anyone they came across in the city of Jerusalem.

- *Are you prepared through your relationship with God to tell others about Jesus? Explain your answer.*

- *Return to the list of individuals you made in the opening lesson. Seek God to help you better prepare yourself to reach out to those on your list. Consider asking God how you may effectively use what he has already done in your life to humbly serve those on your list so they can see the Jesus-in-you in action, not just in words.*

Return Home

- *What did Mary and Joseph do after they had fulfilled the Mosaic law in the temple (Luke 2:39)?*

- *What does Luke tell us about Jesus' development as a child (v. 40)?*

Talking It Out

1. Mary and Joseph were a young, poor, working couple in a non-descript, out-of-the-way village, while Elizabeth and Zechariah were of priestly descent and served in the religious center of Israel in metropolitan Jerusalem. Both couples were serving God even before Gabriel came to them with a remarkable revelation. What does this tell you about the kind of people God can use for his kingdom purposes?

2. God made it possible for a couple past child-bearing years to have a son, and he worked within Mary, a virgin, so she would conceive a miracle child. Review what Gabriel said about these things to Mary (1:35–37). What do such events tell us about the power and faithfulness of God? Can we still count on him to be the same today and tomorrow as he was then? Explain your answer.

3. God's plan to change the world began in the heart of Israel, not in the capital city of the Roman Empire. And his Son was conceived in an insignificant village, in a young Jewish virgin woman, and was born in the shadow of a client king's majestic palace. What does this tell you about how truly significant, monumental change can begin? Are you a change agent? If so, in what way? If not, why?

LESSON 2

Preparation for Ministry

(2:41–4:13)

Luke ends his presentation of the earliest boyhood years of Jesus with the words "The child grew more powerful in grace, for he was being filled with wisdom, and the favor of God was upon him" (2:40). Jesus grew more in whose grace? God's. And he was being filled with whose wisdom? God's. Can we say which Person of the Trinity was doing these things within the boy Jesus? Was it the Father or the Spirit? New Testament scholar Gerald Hawthorne, in his important study *The Presence and the Power*, helps us with this. In his discussion of this passage in Luke, Hawthorne writes:

> Luke does not say in just so many words
> who this agent is. One may infer, however,
> both from what Luke had to say earlier
> about the agent at Jesus' birth (1:35),
> and from what he will say later on about
> the driving force in Jesus' ministry (4:1),
> that this unnamed agent was none other
> than the Holy Spirit. Jesus, therefore, was
> growing strong (in mind) because the Holy
> Spirit was ever more and more filling him
> [with wisdom, *sophia*].[34]

- *Isaiah 11:1–5 is a prophecy about the Messiah. What does verse 2 say about the Holy Spirit and the Messiah? Now compare Isaiah's words to Luke's description of Jesus' growth as a boy. How does Isaiah's prophecy connect to what Luke says?*

- *Proverbs 1:2–7 provides a good sense of what the Bible calls wisdom. So when the Spirit progressively filled Jesus with wisdom, what more, specifically, did Jesus receive?*

- *Have you known any wise individuals? What were they like?*

- *Have you sought to grow in wisdom? If so, what steps have you taken, and what have you learned about wisdom along the way?*

A Glimpse at Twelve

Before Luke turns to the adult Jesus, he gives us another glimpse of Jesus and his family life when the boy was twelve years old, a preteen.

- *Where did Joseph and Mary take Jesus, and why were they there (Luke 2:41–42)?*

- *Luke says that it was the "custom" of Joseph and Mary to take this trip to Jerusalem (v. 42). What does this reveal about their commitment to Judaism and the Mosaic law?*

 DIGGING DEEPER

Hawthorne suggests that this trip may have been Jesus' first one into Jerusalem:

> From the way in which Luke begins this narrative, it is difficult to say with complete certainty whether or not Jesus had previously accompanied Joseph and Mary on any of their annual pilgrimages to Jerusalem to celebrate the feast of Passover. For the following reasons, however, it may be presumed that he had not: (1) The feast of Passover was one of the three feasts that Jewish adult males

originally were ordered by the Law to attend each year (Exod. 23:14; Deut. 16:16), and by New Testament times it was the only annual feast required of those males living at a distance from Jerusalem. (2) It was not expected that women should go up to these feasts, and at an early period the presence of women and children was a matter of controversy. (3) According to Mishnaic regulations, which may very well have been in effect in Jesus' time, boys from the age of thirteen on were obliged to make the pilgrimage to Jerusalem at Passover and take their place among the adult males of the Israelite community. It was customary, however, for a child belonging to a devout family to be brought up to this feast at least a year before his thirteenth birthday in order to acquaint the child with the obligation that was soon to fall upon his shoulders. Hence, it is more likely that this difficult journey to Jerusalem from a village [Nazareth] more than sixty-five miles away was for Jesus, a boy of only twelve years, his very first experience in this sacred city.[35]

- *Did you visit any major metropolitan cities when you were younger? What was that experience like for you? What impact did it have on you as you grew up?*

- *What do you suppose this visit to Jerusalem at twelve years old may have been like for Jesus?*

Luke doesn't get into the details of the Passover, but he does mention something that happened after the festival had ended.

- *What did Joseph and Mary realize about a day's journey out of Jerusalem (Luke 2:43)? What did they do immediately after this discovery (vv. 44–45)?*

- *Where did they finally find their son, and what had he been doing (vv. 46–47)? How did the people who were listening respond to Jesus' interaction with the Jewish teachers? What does this tell you about Jesus' intellectual abilities and his knowledge of Scripture?*

- *How did Jesus' parents respond to their son's absence from the family (v. 48)?*

- *How did Jesus respond to his parents (v. 49)? Note, too, what Jesus said about God as his Father. What does that reveal about Jesus' growing self-perception and its implication for his relationship to his own parents?*

- *Mary and Joseph "didn't fully understand" what Jesus told them (v. 50), but that didn't alter how Jesus responded. Read verses 51–52 and summarize what they say about the rest of Jesus' growing-up years.*

- *Compare verse 52 and verse 40. What do you find in common between the two passages in their description of Jesus and his development?*

Unlike Mark (6:3) and Matthew (13:55), which mention Jesus' trade craft, Luke zeroes in on Jesus' skills in handling Scripture—skills he began to learn as a young boy. As Hawthorne states:

> Between his [Jesus'] birth and the start of his mission, was the time when he learned the Law of God, the Torah. He learned it from his devout parents at home and from the rabbis in his synagogue. He learned to read the Law (cf. Luke 4:16). He worked at memorizing it so that he could quote it with ease (Luke 4:3–13; cf. 2:46–47). He

loved the Law and filled his mind with it. Its message seemed to have gripped him and shaped his thinking and his life. Like the blessed man of Psalm 1, his delight must have been in the Law of the Lord on which he meditated day and night (Ps. 1:2)—inferences that can be drawn from his youthful but intelligent interaction with the teachers of the Torah in the Temple (Luke 2:46–47). These, too, were the years when he formed good habits that were to last a lifetime. Again it is Luke who provides an example of this, for it is he who notes that on the Sabbath Jesus went to the synagogue "as his custom was" (Luke 4:16), as he was in the habit of doing.[36]

EXPERIENCE GOD'S HEART

- *We come to know God in a variety of ways, but we best learn about him and how to follow his Son through his written revelation, the Bible. What are your habits when it comes to learning the Bible?*

- *Do you, as Jesus showed was his personal habit, listen to teachers of Scripture? Why or why not?*

- *Do you ask them "probing questions" (Luke 2:46)? If so, provide some examples.*

- *Do you sometimes amaze your teachers with your understanding and answers (v. 47)? If so, give an example. If not, why do you think this is?*

- *Consider what you can begin doing over the next few weeks that will eventually deepen and widen your understanding of God's Word. Then commit that plan to God, asking him to use it to make you wise as the Spirit joins you in this spiritually maturing work.*

John the Baptizer

Luke began his Gospel by telling about two births: John's and Jesus'. He has now told us about the births of both men, and he has given us some idea of John's growing-up years and more detail about Jesus'. Next he moves into the mission and ministry of John as an adult, what John did to "illuminate the path that leads to the way of peace" (1:79).

- *What came to John, where was he, and when did it come (3:1–2)? Be sure to consult study notes 'a' and 'b' for 3:1–2.*

 # THE BACKSTORY

Luke provides several historical markers to indicate the time period of John the Baptizer's ministry. The first is "Emperor Tiberius, son of Caesar" (3:1–2). Caesar Augustus died on August 19, AD 14. Before he died, he appointed his stepson, Tiberius, to succeed him. Tiberius was a competent general and an able administrator. In the year 26, he appointed Pontius Pilate as governor over Judea, and Pilate is the second of Luke's historical markers. Pilate served as governor from 26 to 36. John's "prophetic commission" (vv. 1–2) came in Tiberius's fifteenth year as emperor, which would have been from August AD 27 to August AD 28.

Luke's third historical marker is Antipas, one of King Herod's sons (vv. 1–2). He was "governor over Galilee" and "the more arid land called Perea, a long narrow strip extending along half of the eastern coast of the Dead Sea and reaching northward along the eastern side of the Jordan almost to the Sea of Galilee."[37] Unlike his father who had the title of king, Antipas received the title of tetrarch, "a less prestigious office than that of a king." He rebuilt the city of Sepphoris and made that his capital city until he finished building the new city of Tiberius in 23, named after the Roman emperor of his day. From Tiberius, he ruled his territories.[38]

Luke's next historical marker is Philip. Also a son of King Herod, Augustus made Philip a tetrarch over the northeastern part of what had been Herod's domain. According to Josephus, Philip was generally well liked by his subjects, and he ruled with moderation and provided peace in the region.[39]

Finally, Luke turns from political leaders to religious leaders to provide his fifth and last historical marker: the time period of two high priests, Annas and Caiaphas (vv. 1–2). "Annas was the high priest from A.D. 6 to A.D. 15 but was deposed by the Roman authorities. Eventually his son-in-law, Caiaphas, was placed in the position (A.D. 18–36). The Jews continued to recognize Annas as the rightful high priest though Caiaphas functioned in that role."[40]

His Overall Message

• *What was John's major message, and what ritual did he link with that message (Luke 3:3)?*

• *What prophecy did John fulfill, and what light does the prophecy cast on his ministry's focus (vv. 4–6)?*

His Central Charge

• *What was John's indictment against those who came to him to be baptized (vv. 7–9)?*

• *What effect did it have on those who came to him (v. 10)?*

- *What did John tell the crowds to do (v. 11)?*

- *What was his counsel to tax collectors (vv. 12–13)?*

- *What did John tell soldiers to do (v. 14)?*

- *Given what Luke describes here as John's ministry, what does a life following repentance look like? To some degree, is repentance specific to groups or individuals? Support your answer from the biblical text.*

Are You the Messiah?

- *What did some people begin to wonder about John, and why did this happen (v. 15)?*

- *What was John's response to this speculation (vv. 16–17)?*

His Arrest

- *John also publicly spoke out against the tetrarch Herod Antipas. What did John say about Antipas, and how did the ruler respond (vv. 18–20)?*

- *Do you think John was wise to make this public critique against Herod Antipas? Why or why not?*

SHARE GOD'S HEART

Sometimes sharing God's heart with other people involves exposing corruption even when it involves political officials. The Hebrew prophets of old did this, and John the Baptizer followed in their footsteps.

- *How might we combine the good news of salvation in Christ with the message of divine judgment on sin and the need for repentance and a changed life?*

- *How can we convey that message of judgment and redemption to political leaders?*

- *Consider what you can do to engage your political leaders with this message in the coming weeks and months. Your leaders may not receive or welcome your message, just as Antipas did not accept John's rebuke. But even its rejection indicates that they heard your message. You must have the courage and conviction to speak the truth whether your hearers accept it or not.*

Baptism and Divine Approval

- *Before John's arrest, Jesus came to him to be baptized, but not because he needed repentance, as John himself testified (vv. 16–17). What happened at Jesus' baptism (vv. 21–22; see also for these verses study notes 'b,' 'c,' and 'd')?*

Why was Jesus baptized? Bible scholar John Martin explains:

> The purpose of the baptism was to anoint Jesus with the Spirit and to authenticate Him by the Father for beginning His ministry. Each Person of the Godhead

was involved in the activity of the Son on earth, including His baptism. The Son was baptized, the Holy Spirit descended on Him, and the Father spoke approvingly of Jesus. In His baptism Jesus identified Himself with sinners though He was not a sinner.[41]

Jesus' Age and Lineage

Luke tells us that Jesus began his ministry when he was "about thirty years old" (vv. 23–38). Do we know how old Jesus actually was? Was he in his late twenties? Or perhaps in his early thirties? Determining his age depends on the year Jesus was born, and this is a matter of calculation and debate. Most of the suggestions range from 7 BC to 4 BC. He could not have been born *after* Herod the Great died in the spring of 4 BC, for this ruler was alive at the time of Jesus' birth. So the latest birth year of Jesus is early 4 BC. But others, such as Corey Piper, put Jesus' birth year in 7 BC, arguing for that date for a number of reasons, most biblical and a few extra-biblical.[42]

If Jesus began his ministry around the fifteenth year of Emperor Tiberius's reign (vv. 1–2), then his ministry started in the year AD 28 or perhaps 29. Doing the math from 7 BC to AD 28 (recognizing that there is no year zero), Jesus' ministry began when he was thirty-five years old. If we figure from a birth year of 4 BC to AD 28, then Jesus was thirty-two years old at the start of his ministry. In either case, Luke's approximation of about thirty years would fit.[43]

- *Luke provides Jesus' lineage. From whom does he trace it (3:23–38)?*

- *With whom does Luke's genealogy end?*

- *Why do you think Luke took his genealogy all the way back in history to the first created man while Matthew (1:2) traced Jesus' lineage only to Abraham?*

Beating the Tests

After Jesus' baptism by John, Jesus, full of the Holy Spirit, went into the wilderness for forty days (Luke 4:1–2).

- *Who led Jesus into the wilderness, and what was the purpose of this exile (vv. 1–2)?*

- *What physical duress did Jesus endure (vv. 1–2)?*

- *In the chart following, summarize in the middle column the traps Satan laid in an attempt to persuade Jesus to sin, and then in the righthand column, summarize Jesus' responses to Satan.*

Passage	Satan's Challenge	Jesus' Answer
4:3–4		
4:5–8		
4:9–12		

- *What was the outcome of this spiritual battle (v. 13)?*

- *In each challenge from Satan, Jesus based his response on Scripture. Review the study notes 'e,' 'i,' and 'k.' From what book of the Bible does Jesus quote each time? What does this tell you about Jesus' knowledge of this book? And since it is the final book of the Pentateuch—what Jews refer to as the Torah—what might Jesus' knowledge of this book suggest about his grasp of the entire Pentateuch?*

- *When you find yourself in spiritual battle, how do you typically engage it? Is one of your weapons Scripture? If so, how do you wield it?*

Talking It Out

1. Reflect on what you have learned about Jesus' life so far. What are some facts that set Jesus apart from his fellow human beings? What are some facts about his young life that are truly ordinary, often found in other human lives as they develop?

2. Jesus' stepfather, Joseph, does not seem to factor into Jesus' life after the temple incident at age twelve. The assumption is that Joseph died, making Mary a widowed parent. Discuss what it's like growing up with one parent. What are some challenges that the children face in single-parent homes? And what are some of the struggles and joys of single parents? Does knowing that Jesus faced the death of a parent help you even better connect with him? If so, why?

3. Why do you think the Spirit purposely led Jesus into the wilderness to be tested by Satan? What do you imagine Jesus learned about himself, God, and the devil through that wilderness experience?

LESSON 3

Jesus Launches His Ministry

(4:14–6:16)

After Jesus' victory over Satan, he left the wilderness and, still empowered by the Spirit, "returned to Galilee." There "his fame spread throughout the region," and he went about teaching in the synagogues. His message and ministry were so amazing that the people "glorified him" (Luke 4:14–15).

The infant, young boy, and teenager had become a man—a man worthy of being heard, a man in whom the Spirit of God rested, strengthened, illuminated, and fellowshipped. Jesus was ready to do his Father's work. As such, he was a man to be reckoned with. To some, he would be a healer. To others, a prophet from God. And to many, the long-awaited Messiah.

But to others, Jesus would be a threat. A man who had to be confronted, whose popularity had to be squelched. He would be misunderstood and sometimes understood all too well. Some would even want him arrested, imprisoned, and killed.

He had become a man about whom no one could be neutral. He, even more than John the Baptizer, evoked the need to respond. He was someone individuals had to make decisions about.

Who was he?

Why was he here?

By whose authority and power did he speak, heal, and drive out demons?

His life, ministry, and message demanded answers. Jesus knew this, and he was ready for what was to come.

Hometown Rejection

Nazareth was Jesus' hometown (4:16–17). His family, friends, and neighbors were there. They had been with him as he grew into a man. They knew what he was like, including how well he performed the craft that his father had trained him to do. They were quite familiar with him. How would those who knew him best respond to him?

- *Where did Jesus go in Nazareth, and what did he do (vv. 16–21)?*

- *When Jesus said, "Today, these Scriptures came true in front of you" (v. 21), what exactly was Jesus claiming about himself? Go back to the passage that he read from Isaiah. What does it say about the person it describes?*

- *How did the people in the synagogue respond to what Jesus read and claimed (v. 22)?*

- *Read verses 23–27. What did Jesus say to the hometown crowd? What was the heart of his reply?*

- *How did those who knew him best answer him (vv. 28–29)?*
  Be sure to consult study note 'b' for verse 28.

- *What do you make of their response? Do you think it was*
  justified? Why or why not?

- *What, then, happened with Jesus? What did he do (vv. 30–31)?*

- *Have you ever been rejected by family, friends, neighbors,*
  or work associates because of your Christian faith?
  How does what happened to Jesus help you handle the
  rejection you experienced?

Jesus had made it clear that his ministry would include gentiles, not just Jews. He was God's prophet, to be sure, but he was a prophet for all peoples, not just for God's chosen nation. Even Israel's own history demonstrated God's concern for all peoples—a truth that those who knew Jesus best were unwilling to accept. But did they reject Jesus for this only? No. They also seem to turn away from him *because* he claimed to be a prophet (v. 24). His hometown was unwilling to see him filling this divinely appointed role. To them, Jesus may have been a good guy, even a great guy, but he was not a spokesman for God, and he was too generous in his focus for conducting God's work. To them, Jesus had insulted them, and they were willing to make him pay with his life.

So Jesus left Nazareth and traveled to the city of Capernaum. As far as we know, Jesus never returned to his hometown.

Conquering Demons and Illnesses

Capernaum was on the western shore of the Sea of Galilee (Matthew 4:13). It was large enough to be called a city, and it had its own synagogue—"a synagogue built by the centurion of the detachment of Roman soldiers that appears to have been quartered in the place" (Luke 7:1–5; Matthew 8:5–9).[44] Capernaum was also the place where Matthew had a "tax-collecting station" (Matthew 9:9). And this city became Jesus' headquarters for his ministry, at least in the region of Galilee (4:13).

- *What did Jesus do in this city, and how was he received (Luke 4:31–32)?*

One thing that amazed the people about Jesus' teaching was that he spoke with "great authority." Commenting on this, Leon Morris states:

> Originality was not highly prized among the rabbis and it was usual to accredit one's words by citing illustrious predecessors. For example, R. Eliezer piously disavowed novelty: 'nor have I ever in my life said a thing which I did not hear from my teachers' (*Sukkah* 28a; a similar statement is made about R. Johanan b. Zakki, and the attitude was common). Jesus did no such thing, and the authority with which he spoke impressed people.[45]

- *Have you ever heard a speaker or teacher present their material without leaning on other human authorities? If not, why do you think this is so? If you have, did you find this person credible? Why or why not?*

- *While Jesus was teaching, what happened (vv. 33–35)?*

- *What did the demon indicate that he knew about Jesus (v. 34)? Has Luke given any indication yet that the people who heard Jesus speak knew as much as the demon knew about him?*

- *How did the people in the synagogue respond to Jesus (vv. 36–37)?*

- *Where did Jesus go, and what did he do after he left the synagogue (vv. 38–44)?*

- *Why do you think Jesus searched out a "secluded place" and stayed there for a while (v. 42)?*

- *What value do you place in getting rest from your labors? Do you feel as if you get enough? Why or why not?*

Fish and Fishers of Men

- *In the next event that Luke describes, Jesus was "preaching to a crowd on the shore of Lake Galilee" (5:1). What happened there (vv. 1–7)?*

- *Tell about the exchange between Simon Peter and Jesus and what Simon and the other fishermen decided to do at Jesus' invitation (vv. 8–11).*

- *What do you think these fishermen saw in Jesus that led them to leave their career behind to follow him?*

EXPERIENCE GOD'S HEART

- *Have you given up anything to follow Jesus? If so, what or whom?*

- *Has the sacrifice been worth it? Explain your answer.*

- *Do you sense that you need to give up anything else? If so, what?*

Healing and Blasphemy Charges

In an unnamed city, Jesus encountered "a man covered with leprous sores" (Luke 5:12).

> *Leprosy* in biblical times was the name given to a variety of diseases, some curable and some not. In its worse form it was a greatly dreaded and very dreadful disease. It was both disfiguring and fatal and the ancient world's only defence against it was quarantine (Lev. 13:46). Sufferers were forbidden to approach other people, and to prevent accidental contact they

were required to call out 'Unclean' (Lev. 13:45). They had no way of earning a living and had to depend on charity. The psychological effects of all this seem to have been as serious as the physical... It [leprosy] was defiling. People were ashamed of it, though it was no fault of their own.[46]

• *What was the leper's request of Jesus, and how did Jesus meet it (Luke 5:13–14)?*

• *Describe the spread of Jesus' fame and what he did in the midst of it (vv. 15–16).*

• *Do you find times and places to pray even when your life is full and busy? If not, why? How has that been working out for you? If you do pray often, what have you noticed about how your life goes?*

Not everyone appreciated, much less felt awed, by what Jesus said and did. Some even found his actions deeply offensive.

- *Read verses 17–26. Summarize what happened, including noting who responded favorably to Jesus, who did not, and why.*

- *What connection did Jesus make between physical healing and the forgiveness of a sinner? Why did the religious leaders find forgiveness so offensive?*

- *What did Jesus prove about himself?*

SHARE GOD'S HEART

Jesus had no qualms about providing evidence for who he was and why he acted the way he did. In fact, in this instance, he volunteered evidence before anyone asked him for it. He knew what the religious leaders were thinking, and he knew how easy it would be to voice forgiveness without showing that he had the divine authority to grant it. So he set up the test, and then he met the hardest part of it: healing a paraplegic (vv. 21–25). His action proved his authority.

- *What are you able and willing to do to show others that Christ abides in you and that he is and can do what he claims?*

Evidence can come in many forms, including in our testimony about our relationship with Jesus; historical evidence about the life, death, and resurrection of Jesus; reasons for accepting Scripture as the Word of God; miracles God has performed in your life or in the life of someone you know; and even answers you have received through prayer.

- *Do you know someone who questions who Jesus claimed to be, whether he even lived and performed the deeds that the Gospels describe, or anything else about Jesus the Christ? What is this person's objection, and why do you think they feel that way?*

- *Do you have evidence you can use to answer this person's objections? If not, consult with another Christian about this person's issues and how you can address them. Check out one or more of the resources we list in the endnote.[47] Good answers are available if you know where to find them.*

- *Once you have some answers, seek out this person and prayerfully and gently share what you found. They may not respond to you as you hope, but God can still use your efforts to lead them closer to him.*

Winning a Tax Collector

- *After healing the man who was paralyzed, whom did Jesus seek out, and what was this man's occupation (v. 27)?*

- *What did Jesus offer him, and what was the man's response (vv. 28–29)?*

- *Did Jesus accept this man's invitation, and what happened as a result (vv. 29–32)?*

- *Jesus distinguished between the so-called righteous and "those who know they are sinners" (v. 32). Was he claiming that some people are truly outside of the category of sinner and therefore are righteous—that is, just or morally right in their character and in their actions? Support your answer.*

- *What does Jesus' answer tell you about how he saw Matthew, the tax collector? What does the criticism of the "Jewish religious leaders and experts of the law" (vv. 29–30) reveal about their attitude and approach to people like Matthew? Which view depicts the one that we should take toward our fellow human beings?*

- *At this same event, the religious leaders continued challenging Jesus. Summarize their criticism and Jesus' answer (vv. 33–39).*

- *Verse 39 contains the key to Jesus' wine analogy. What are the "old ways" that the religious leaders believed were better to follow? How can such "old ways" be a hindrance to considering new teaching and new ways of living?*

- *Are there old ways of thinking and living that are holding you back from following Jesus fully? If so, what are some of them? What does Jesus encourage you to be open to tasting—that is, to embracing and experiencing?*

Sabbath Traditions

Next Luke records two incidents, both of which took place on days of the Sabbath. Both illustrate how "old ways" got in the way of what Jesus believed, taught, and lived.

- *Read 6:1–2. Describe what Jesus and his disciples did on the Sabbath and how that drew the ire of some Jewish religious leaders.*

- *Now consider Jesus' response to his critics (vv. 3–5), including reading about the incident that Jesus refers to as told in 1 Samuel 21:1–6. Summarize Jesus' response. Then explain how he can claim to be "master over the Sabbath" (Luke 6:5).*

- *In the second Sabbath incident, Jesus is teaching in the synagogue (Luke 6:6). Retell what happens and how the people received what Jesus did (vv. 6–11).*

- *Have you ever done something that was good and had people criticize or reject you for it? Tell what happened. What has been the fallout for you?*

Singling Out the Twelve

Luke tells us that, after the last synagogue incident he described, Jesus went away and spent the entire night in prayer (v. 12). At the start of the next day, Jesus selected twelve from among his disciples to be "his apostles" (v. 13). From this point on in history, they would be known as the Twelve.

- *Read study note 'd' for Luke 6:13, and then summarize what an apostle is.*

- *Consult a Bible dictionary, Bible encyclopedia, or an online resource to find information about each member of the Twelve (vv. 14–16). Jot down next to each person named what you learned about that individual.*

Simon Peter

Andrew

Jacob

John

Philip

Bartholomew

Matthew

Thomas

Jacob the son of Alpheus

Simon the Zealot

Judah

Judas

- *Now look over your notes on these apostles. Remember, Jesus selected them after a night of prayer, indicating that he knew each of these was his Father's choice for the role of an apostle. What are some conclusions you would draw about this selection?*

Jesus' Ministry So Far

As we've seen so far, Jesus evoked a response. Some individuals chose to follow him. Others were amazed by him and his teaching and miracles of healing and exorcism but may not have become his disciples. Others found him irritating, off-putting, offensive, and even blasphemous. Some even ran him out of town and tried to kill him. Even the good he did could provoke public criticism, challenges, and anger.

Jesus was not a neutral figure. He brought out what people harbored inside, and what they revealed usually had more to say about them and their condition than it did about Jesus.

We're early in Luke's Gospel still, and he has much more to tell us about Jesus. The story, as it unfolds, will continue to show the power, authority, empathy, and compassion of Jesus, the Son of Man and Son of God, the Messiah the Scriptures had promised would come. But he was not the kind of Messiah the people expected. He was far better! At least he was to those who had eyes to see and ears to hear.

Talking It Out

1. When you first learned about Jesus, do you recall what you thought about him? What led you to change your perception of him and your response to him?

2. Truth always has its enemies, as does good. Jesus, as John says in his Gospel, is the way, the truth, and the life (John 14:6). While many will be drawn to him, many will find him repellent and will despise him. What can you learn about Jesus' way of dealing with critics that can help you do the same in your life? What can you learn about the reactions to him that can help you face them and process them, whether they are positive or negative?

3. What have you learned so far about Jesus, his message, and his ways that can help you navigate the expectations of others in your city, church, or culture? How should you live even when you know that what you do will draw criticism and antagonism?

LESSON 4

Life Teaching, Faith, and John

(6:17–7:50)

Jesus was a rabbi—a Jewish teacher. He had students (that's what the disciples were) who followed him and sat at his feet to learn and watch how he lived so they could learn how to live like him.

This pedagogical model has ancient roots, going all the way back to Moses' relationship with Joshua, Eli's ways with Samuel, and Elijah's teacher-student relationship with Elisha. In Jesus' day, the model was commonplace, including among the Pharisees.

A rabbi's "disciples not only 'followed' their teacher literally as he walked or rode on a donkey in front, but they also 'walked' after him morally."[48] They wanted to live as he lived, to make choices as he did, to be like him as much as they could. After all, he was the expert, and he was among the learned of the Torah. If you wanted to live as God wanted, you had to know and obey the Torah. And the ones who knew the Torah best were the rabbis. So disciples listened to their teacher's instruction, asked their teacher questions, observed what their teacher did, and sought to imitate him. As one Bible scholar put it:

> The pupil had to absorb all the traditional
> wisdom with 'eyes, ears and every
> member' by seeking the company of a
> Rabbi, by serving him, following him, and
> imitating him and not only by listening to

him. The task of the pupil is therefore not
only to hear but also to see. The pupil is a
witness to his teacher's words; he is also a
witness to his actions as well. He does not
only say 'I heard my teacher' but also 'I
saw my teacher do this or that'.[49]

Jesus had now chosen who his closest disciples would be, and
so he led them "down from the hillside to a level field, where a
large number of his [other] disciples waited, along with a massive
crowd" (Luke 6:17).

- *Where was the large crowd from (v. 17)? See if you can
  locate these places on a map that shows what Palestine
  was like in Jesus' day.*

- *Why had all the people come, and what initially
  happened (vv. 18–19)? From which Person of the Trinity
  do you suppose this "supernatural power" came?*

Sermon on the Plain

Jesus spoke a great deal, and like any speaker or teacher, he
repeated some of the same material while inserting new subjects and emphases, depending on what he believed his audience
needed. Scholars have observed that Jesus' talk here in Luke
has some similarities to his sermon in Matthew 5–7, but there
are important differences too. While the sermons recorded in

Luke and Matthew "are addressed to disciples, begin with beatitudes, conclude with the same parables, and have generally the same content...in Luke the 'Jewish parts' of the sermon (i.e., the interpretation of the Law) are omitted."[50] Given that Luke's initial readership was gentile and Jewish, it seems reasonable that his Gospel would contain less on the meaning of the Torah than would Matthew's Gospel, which is more Jewish focused. It's also the case that Jesus, as a preeminent speaker and teacher, would adjust his content to the needs of his audience, which in the case recorded by Luke included gentiles, not just Jews.

- *Jesus directed his talk to "his followers" (Luke 6:20). Imagine you were among the crowd but not one of Jesus' disciples. What might it have been like to hear a great teacher but not yet be counted among his students? How might you have felt?*

- *Jesus opened his sermon with a contrast between the blessed and the sorrowful (vv. 20–26). Summarize these contrasts in the chart that follows:*

The Blessed	The Sorrowful

• *What did Jesus say that surprised you? Why?*

• *Jesus made such a contrast to call his disciples to follow the path of the blessed. Did Jesus make this path seem easy or challenging? Explain your answer.*

• *Love (and its characteristics of forgiveness, compassion, and service) was one of Jesus' primary themes. In verses 27–36, Jesus talked about how to love one's enemies. First read through these verses and write down what you learn about whom Jesus regarded as personal enemies. What are our enemies like, and what do they seek to do against us?*

• *Second, go back through those verses and jot down how differently we are to treat those who are our enemies. What are we to be like, and what are we supposed to do?*

- *Now return to these verses one more time. What reasons did Jesus give for being loving toward our enemies? Why should we treat them differently rather than the way they treat us?*

- *Judging and criticizing others was the next topic Jesus addressed (vv. 37–42). Summarize (1) what Jesus did not want his followers to do and then (2) what positive actions he wanted his students to take.*

- *Next Jesus talked about good fruit versus bad fruit (vv. 43–45). What does bad fruit symbolize and from where does it come? What does good fruit symbolize and from where does it come?*

- *In relationship to our character (who we are) and actions (what we do), what do our actions reveal about our character?*

- *Jesus closed his time of instruction with a call to not just know what he taught but to put it into practice (vv. 46–49). What is the person like who knows and does what Jesus taught? What is the person like who knows what Jesus taught but refuses to obey it?*

EXPERIENCE GOD'S HEART

- *Jesus ended with a question, a call to action, a call to commitment. What is your answer to his question? What can you do even today to not just see and hear what Jesus said but to imitate him and live the life he lived?*

- *You can't live his life in your own power any more than he did in his human nature. He was empowered by the Holy Spirit, and you must be as well. As a man, Jesus lived in dependence on the Spirit and his Father, remaining in communion with them through prayer, solitude, study of the Law, and other spiritual disciplines. How do you remain connected to God?[51]*

- *Since we also learn in community as Jesus' first disciples did, whom do you know who might help you learn and apply some of the spiritual disciplines to your life so you can live as Jesus did? Now make a plan that involves meeting with this person or group to walk in Christ together, fellow disciples of the greatest teacher of all time.*

Gentile Faith and Healing

After his time of teaching, Jesus returned to his homebase of Capernaum (7:1).

- *What happened there (7:2–10)? Summarize your findings.*

- *Whom did Jesus commend and why?*

- *What did this person receive as a result of his great faith in Jesus?*

- *The person who received a miracle from Jesus was a Roman military captain, a gentile leader. What was his reputation among the Jews in Capernaum, and what were some indications that he deserved that reputation?*

- *What are you known for, including among those who might be inclined to dislike you? What evidence would you point to that supports your answer?*

Death Overcome

After Jesus left Capernaum, he traveled to a village called Nain (v. 11). Nain had a wall around it, and the town was located about five miles southeast of Nazareth, Jesus' hometown, and about twenty-five miles southwest of Capernaum.[52]

- *Who traveled with Jesus to Nain (v. 11)?*

- *What and whom did they come upon near Nain (v. 12)?*

- *What was Jesus' response to what he saw, and what resulted from what he did (vv. 13–17)?*

- *What does this event reveal about Jesus and his view of life and death?*

John in Focus

Luke now turns his attention from Jesus to John the Baptizer. At the start of his Gospel, Luke told about two miraculous conceptions: the conception of John to a couple beyond childbearing age and the conception of Jesus within a virgin. John has not come into the picture since Luke described his ministry and Jesus' baptism. And when Luke last spoke of John, John had been arrested by the tetrarch Herod Antipas and locked up in prison for speaking the truth about Antipas (3:19–20).

As the news spread about Jesus, John's disciples "reported to him in prison about all the wonderful miracles and the works Jesus was doing" (7:18). This led John to send two of his disciples to Jesus to verify that what he had initially believed about Jesus was, in fact, true (vv. 19–21).

Jesus to John

- *What did Jesus do before he gave an answer to John's disciples (v. 21)?*

- *What did Jesus tell John's disciples (vv. 22–23)?*

- *Now explain why Jesus performed deeds before presenting a verbal response. What is the link between his actions and his words?*

- *Return to Jesus' sermon on the plain (6:20–49). Reread the sermon and jot down anything you find there that supports the connection Jesus made to John's disciples between one's words and one's deeds and what that connection reveals about the kind of person one is.*

❤ SHARE GOD'S HEART

Jesus linked the truth about his identity to his service to others. If we are his followers, his genuine disciples, then we need to do likewise. As Jesus said in another context, "I give you now a new commandment: Love each other just as much as I have loved you. For when you demonstrate the same love I have for you by loving one another, everyone will know that you're my true followers" (John 13:34–35). If we are truly Christians, then we will love others as Christ did.

- *Do you love others as Christ has loved you? If so, how do your deeds show it? If not, why?*

- *What is at least one love habit you can build into your life that will demonstrate to others that you are a Christ-follower? Who could use that love habit expressed toward them? Bathe your time in prayer for that person or group, asking God to help you learn how to express Christian love to them so they will know that you are Christ's disciple.*

Jesus on John

After John's disciples left Jesus to take his answer back to their teacher, Jesus turned to the crowd that had gathered around him and spoke to them about John (Luke 7:24).

- *What did Jesus say about John (vv. 24–28)?*

- *Who embraced what Jesus said as the truth, and who did not? Why did these groups come to different conclusions (vv. 29–30)?*

- *Have you noticed that what often separates people who disagree over an issue or person is their openness to that issue or person? Can you provide an example? Why do you think one's openness can have such a strong influence?*

- *Next Jesus made his comments about John even more personal by talking about the generation of the people standing before him (vv. 31–35). Summarize what he said about them and their critique of John and himself.*

- *In your estimation, were the people right about either John or Jesus? Support your answer.*

- *To what or whom did Jesus point as the vindication of God's wisdom? Why do you think this was the evidence he directed people to?*

Forgiveness at Simeon's Place

The next event Luke describes is a gathering for dinner at the home of a religious leader named Simeon. Simeon was a Pharisee as the New Living Translation makes clear: "One of the Pharisees asked Jesus to have dinner with him, so Jesus went to his home and sat down to eat" (v. 36). Why Simeon invited Jesus to dinner is left unsaid. Some scholars think Simeon did this in order to find a way to trap Jesus, to expose him as a fraud (see vv. 39, 49). One thing we know for sure is that Simeon failed (purposely?) to perform a custom for Jesus that he likely provided for his other guests.

> It was the custom of the day when one had
> a dinner party to provide for the guests'
> feet to be cleaned before the meal. Because
> most roads were unpaved and the normal
> foot attire was sandals, it was common
> for people's feet to be dusty or muddy. As
> pointed out later in the episode, [Simeon]
> did not provide for Jesus' feet to be cleaned
> at the beginning of the dinner party (v. 44).[53]

- *What unexpected event happened while Jesus was dining with other guests at Simeon's house (vv. 37–38)?*

- *What was Simeon's reaction, especially his conclusion about Jesus (v. 39)?*

- *Jesus could tell what Simeon was thinking, so he explained to Simeon in a parable what the woman had done and why Jesus had reacted to her as he did. Summarize the story Jesus told and Simeon's response to Jesus' question (vv. 41–43).*

- *After Jesus commended Simeon's reluctant response (v. 43), Jesus then talked to Simeon about the woman and the motives for her actions (vv. 44–47). Summarize what Jesus said, noting the comparison he made between the woman's actions and those of Simeon.*

- *What did Jesus then say to the woman (vv. 48, 50)?*

- *Did the other dinner guests grasp what Jesus had done (v. 49)? Support your answer.*

Not everyone believed in Jesus, much less accepted that what he taught was true. The same is true today. Some will believe, and some will not. Some will believe quickly, many will come to believe after a long period of time, and some will reject him no matter what. In Jesus' own day, even religious leaders were among those who refused him. Many of those who should have known the Messiah when they saw him, heard him, watched him, challenged him, and received his profound and substantiated answers still refused to embrace him, still refused to follow him.

Nothing has changed. Each of us must decide for ourselves who we believe Jesus is. Through his followers, he has left us with testimony after testimony of his veracity and trustworthiness. But we can still turn our backs on him and walk away.

Nevertheless, if we say we are his followers, then follow him we must. And that requires that we obey his teaching—not just learn it in our heads but follow it in our hearts and in our ways.

Talking It Out

1. Return to what Jesus taught his disciples in Luke 6:20–49. What among his instructions did you find the most challenging, the most illuminating, or the most relevant for today? Explain your answer.

2. Have you had a John-like person in your life—someone who prepared the way for you to accept Jesus by faith? There may have even been more than one person. Tell the group about this individual and recount what this person did to pave the way to Jesus for you.

3. What do you hope others see in you and your life that would draw them to Jesus? You may also want to ask others you know if they see anything in you and your life that they would describe as Christlike and what that is. Many times, people see characteristics in us that we don't see in ourselves. What others say may be encouraging to you.

LESSON 5

Parables, Power, and Provision

(8:1–9:27)

Jesus didn't work alone. The Spirit empowered him, disciples accompanied him and extended his ministry, and many women supported him, including financially. Luke wants us to know that effective ministry, even Jesus', is never a solitary effort. Each of us serves God, but he never leaves us to serve without him, nor does he want us to serve without human help. The ministry of God's own Son demonstrates this.

Traveling Companions

- *Luke summarizes Jesus' ministry message (Luke 8:1).
  What was it?*

- *Who traveled with Jesus, and how did they help him (vv. 1–3)?*

- *Among the named individuals was "Joanna, the wife of Chusa, who managed King Herod's household" (v. 3). Who might Chusa have been in Herod Antipas's administration (see study note 'd' for this verse)?*

⌖ DIGGING DEEPER

Luke had already named the Twelve, all of which were men. At the start of the eighth chapter of his Gospel, Luke names several women who traveled with Jesus and supported him in various ways. Highlighting the efforts of women this way was quite significant. As Garland points out: "To have women disciples 'was unheard-of' in this era…Women were expected to stay at home as much as possible and to avoid men, even relatives. Men were not to be alone with them or to speak with them on the street (see John 4:9, 27)."[54]

Whether in Jewish or gentile society, women were not highly honored or respected in Jesus' day. Scholar Charles Carlston wrote about how women were regarded in Greco-Roman society:

> On balance…the picture drawn is a grim one. Women, if we were to trust the ancient wisdom, are basically ineducable and empty-headed; vengeful, dangerous, and responsible for men's sins; mendacious, treacherous, and unreliable; fickle; valuable only through their relationships with men; incapable of moderation or spontaneous goodness; at their best in the dark; interested only in sex—unless they are with their own husbands, in which case (apparently) they would rather talk. In short, women are one

all 'a set of vultures,' the 'most beastly' of all
the beasts on land or sea, and marriage is at
best a necessary evil.[55]

In Jewish society, the treatment of women wasn't much better. Among Jews, "where the basic unit of society was the family, the status and worth of a woman were directly related to her place in the family...A married woman's role was essentially that of a homemaker and a mother, with her praise coming through the wisdom, influence, and exploits of her husband and sons... Israelite society was dominated by the male."[56] In the synagogues, women were separated from the men by a screen, and they were not allowed to take part in the service. They had to sit and listen, not speak. In the Jewish family, the male head instructed the family in the Law and led his family in worship.

In contrast, Jesus in his ministry acknowledged, honored, and respected women. He didn't try to hide them away but included them among his ministry team. He raised the status of women and showed their intrinsic worth by assuming they could learn and therefore teaching them, by ministering to them in multiple ways, by allowing them to travel with him and learn alongside men, by ministering to their family members, and by responding to their calls for help. And all of this in a culture that was led by men and that disdained women.

New Testament scholar Leon Morris adds another thought about women in the Gospels' accounts: "It is worth reflecting that the Gospels record no woman as ever taking action against him [Jesus]: his enemies were all men."[57] Many men found Jesus threatening, while women typically did not.

- *From what you've studied in Luke's Gospel so far,
  what reasons can you see for men to find Jesus more
  threatening than women did?*

- *If you are a woman, how well have you been received into ministry? Have any men created roadblocks for you? If so, why? If not, why do you think this is so?*

Kingdom Illustrations

Luke turns to providing an illustration Jesus used when he taught the people who came to hear him (Luke 8:4). Jesus then unpacked the story's meaning to his disciples and encouraged them through a metaphor.

Parable of the Seed

- *Read the parable of the seed in Luke 8:5–8 as well as Jesus' explanation of the parable in verses 11–15. Then fill out the following chart:*

The Four Soil Types	What Happened with the Seeds	Jesus' Explanation of the Soil and the Seeds

- *Which soil type and seed growth do you believe best describes your own response to God's Word?*

- *Sandwiched between the parable of the seed and Jesus' explanation of it, Luke tells us how Jesus explained the parables to his closest disciples. Summarize what he said about them (vv. 9–10).*

🔊 EXPERIENCE GOD'S HEART

How we receive God's Word depends on the condition of our hearts. Often, references to the human heart in Scripture designate our inner selves—what and how we think, feel, choose, value—in short, all that makes us a person. It includes our spiritual dimension as well: our responsiveness or unresponsiveness to God.[58] So our hearts can be open to God or closed, soft or hard, pliable or unbendable.

- *What is the condition of your heart, especially toward God and his written revelation?*

- *Would others who know you describe you similarly? Why or why not?*

Metaphor of Light-Bearers

Jesus continued speaking to his disciples and this time encouraged them with a metaphor about light and that which it uses to shine forth (vv. 16–18).

- *What will be revealed and to whom?*

- *What should the receivers of the revelation do to prepare for it?*

- *What is the cost of having a closed heart?*

Family of Families

- *While our natural families are important, Jesus made it clear that there is another family that's even more important, a kind of family of families. What is this greater family (vv. 19–21)?*

- *What characterizes these greater family members?*

Morris puts Jesus' teaching here in perspective:

> Those who are near to Jesus are those who take seriously their duty to God. This does not mean that family ties are unimportant or can be ignored: Jesus is not disowning his family. He thought of his mother even when he hung on the cross in the agony of achieving the world's redemption (John 19:26f.). His meaning is that our duty to God takes precedence of all else.[59]

Are you a doer of God's teaching or just a hearer? Jesus makes it clear that his spiritual family consists of those "who long to hear God's words *and* put them into practice" (Luke 8:21, emphasis added).

Comprehensive Authority

In several instances, Jesus demonstrated his authority and power over the natural world, the demonic world, the medical world, and even death itself. The witnesses and recipients of these deeds responded in different ways, each showing the condition of their hearts, especially in relationship to Jesus.

The Natural World

- *Read Luke 8:22–25. Summarize what happens when Jesus decides to cross the lake, including how the disciples respond to Jesus.*

- *Have you ever found yourself in a life-and-death situation? Explain what happened.*

- *Did you appeal to God in the midst of the situation? Why or why not?*

- *What do you think the disciples should have done that would have exhibited their trust in Jesus?*

The World of the Demonic

After crossing the Sea of Galilee, Jesus and his disciples stepped into gentile territory, "the land of the Gerasenes" (v. 26). Here pigs were raised, animals that Jews disdained.

- *Whom did Jesus and his disciples encounter? Describe the man and his condition and what he did when he faced Jesus (vv. 26–29).*

- *Did this man seem in control of himself (vv. 29–31)? Support your answer.*

- *What did the demons believe about Jesus? Who did they think he was, and what did they fear he would do to them (vv. 29–31)?*

- *What did the demons ask Jesus to do, and what was the result (vv. 32–33, 35)?*

- *What did the pig herders do, and how did the townspeople react (vv. 34–37)?*

- *How did the formerly demon-possessed man then respond to Jesus (vv. 38–39)?*

- *What does this incident reveal about demons' beliefs about Jesus?*

- *Does this incident show that one can have a fairly accurate understanding of Jesus and yet remain uncommitted to him? Support your answer.*

Suffering and Death

Jesus then returned to Galilee, where he was met by crowds overjoyed to see him again (v. 40).

- *Who came up to Jesus, and what did he want (vv. 41–42)?*

- *As Jesus followed the man, what happened to interrupt their journey (vv. 43–48)?*

- *What do you think was the source of the surge of healing power that flowed from Jesus (vv. 44–46)?*

- *What was the reason for the release of this power (vv. 47–48)?*

- *Jesus then received another interruption. Who came to him, and what information did he have for Jairus (v. 49)?*

- *What comforting words did Jesus offer to Jairus (v. 50)?*

- *Summarize what occurred once Jesus arrived at the house of Jairus (vv. 51–56).*

- *How did Jairus and his wife respond to the miracle that Jesus performed (vv. 55–56)?*

- *Has God ever intervened in your life in a way that caught you off guard, leaving you surprised and amazed? Tell what happened.*

Authority Shared

Jesus reached a point in his ministry when he decided it was time for his disciples to experience for themselves the things they had seen their Teacher do.

• *What mission did Jesus give his disciples, and how did he equip them (9:1–2)?*

• *Jesus added some specific instructions regarding how they were to carry out their mission. What did he tell them (vv. 3–5)?*

• *What results did the disciples see while they were engaged on their mission (v. 6)?*

❤ SHARE GOD'S HEART

Christian ministry is service toward others. Jesus taught, healed, calmed storms, exorcised demons, answered questions, challenged criticisms, raised the dead, and so much more—all activities geared toward serving others. If we are to follow him and be doers, not just hearers, we must live our lives in service to others as well.

- *What does your Christian service look like? How do you serve others?*

- *If you are not serving others, why?*

- *What can you do to further your service for Christ? Specify at least one action you can take over the next few weeks that can improve or expand your Christian service.*

A Perplexed Tetrarch

Luke now refers back to Herod Antipas, the tetrarch who governed Galilee and had imprisoned John for speaking out about the ruler's misdeeds (9:7; cf. 3:19–20).

- *What had Herod Antipas heard that so confused him (9:7–9)?*

- *What do you learn about John's fate that Luke had not previously mentioned (v. 9)?*

Feeding Thousands

- *Read verses 10–17 and summarize the story.*

- *Now prayerfully reflect on this story and draw out some insights and applications that you can start putting into practice.*

Identity, Destiny, and Discipleship

Jesus had now spent a lot of time with his students. He had taught them, enlightened them, exemplified in his own life what he taught them, performed miracles of healing, exorcism, and resuscitation,[60] and answered criticisms and questions. Now he turns to his students, his own disciples, and asks them about his identity—who, in fact, he is.

- *What did Jesus first ask his disciples, and what did they answer him (vv. 18–19)?*

- *How do their answers compare with the information that Herod Antipas wrestled with in verses 7–9?*

- *What was the second question that Jesus posed to his followers, and what answer did Peter provide (v. 20)?*

- *What was Jesus' immediate response to Peter's declaration (vv. 21–22)?*

- *Jesus then used the revelation about his destiny to further instruct his disciples about how they should live. What did he tell them (vv. 23–25)?*

- *What warning did he give them (v. 26)?*

- *What did he then promise those who were with him at that moment (v. 27)?*

DIGGING DEEPER

When Jesus mentioned cross-bearing, he referred to crucifixion and used it to graphically illustrate the kind of life he expected his disciples to live. He did not rehearse how horrible and painful crucifixion was. Instead, Jesus focused on what it signified: self-surrender and self-sacrifice to Jesus, God's chosen Messiah.

> When the Roman Empire crucified a criminal or captive, the victim was often forced to carry his cross part of the way to the crucifixion site. Carrying his cross through the heart of the city was supposed to be a tacit admission that the Roman Empire was correct in the sentence of death imposed on him, an admission that Rome was right and he was wrong. So when Jesus enjoined his followers to carry their crosses and follow Him, He was referring to a public display before others that Jesus was right and that the disciples were following Him even to their deaths.[61]

We can live to ourselves or live to Jesus Christ. If we do the former, we will lose our soul. If we do the latter, we will gain all that Christ has for us in his kingdom. Put another way, we can continue to live as rebels against the Lord, or we can lay down our arms, surrender our everything to him, and live his way with all the resources he gives us. As rebels, we will one day get what we have fought for—a condemned life forever lived apart from the Source of all life and love. But if we switch sides and give him our loyalty, dedicating our everything to him, he, in turn, will give us "the full riches of everlasting salvation. Submit to Christ and you will get more than you could ever dream or imagine, including a fully glorified, richly renewed you. Keep rebelling against Christ, and you will end up with nothing, not even your soul."[62]

- *To whom are you living your life—to yourself or to Christ?*

- *If you are living to yourself, then take this opportunity to lay aside your rebellion and pledge your life to Jesus. Ask God to forgive you of your sins and then ask him to save you through his Son, Jesus Christ.*

- *If you are living to Christ, then take this time to praise him and thank him for all he has done in you and through you so far, and then renew your commitment to him, asking him to continue to make you more like him and to be effective for him.*

Talking It Out

1. Jesus asked his disciples who those not following him thought he was. What are some of the views that non-Christians have about Jesus today? What can we do to help people better understand who Jesus really was and is?

2. Jesus was teaching the truth, living the truth, and serving others in ways that had the imprint of God's unmatched activity. And yet Jesus predicted that he would greatly suffer, face rejection, and be killed, even though he would come back to life "on the third day" (Luke 9:22). Why was he despised so much?

3. If Jesus could be hated and rejected, can his followers be too? What could lead others to be hostile toward us simply because we identify as followers of Christ?

4. What, if anything, can we do to help alleviate some of the hostility toward us? Or is this simply part of the cost of following Jesus?

LESSON 6

From Transfiguration to Prayer

(9:28–11:13)

Jesus made a promise in Luke 9:27—namely, that some of his disciples at that time would witness "the presence and the power of God's kingdom realm." Eight days later, he fulfilled that promise with Peter, Jacob, and John (v. 28).

Glory Revealed

- *Where did Jesus take these three disciples, and what did he do before their eyes (v. 28)?*

- *How did Jesus' appearance change (v. 29; see also study note 'e')?*

• *Who appeared with Jesus then? Where were they from, and what did they talk about with him (vv. 30–31, 33; see also study note 'f')?*

• *What did Peter want to do for Jesus and the two who appeared with him, and what happened instead (vv. 33–35)?*

• *What occurred when the glorious event came to a close (v. 36)?*

• *Given what the text says about this event, what would you conclude was its purpose? Why was Jesus transfigured—to achieve what? Bear in mind that this revelation of his glory and Sonship may have served multiple purposes.*

Faith and the Demonic

After the light of the Father and his Son shone so brightly on the mountain, Jesus and his three disciples descended the heights and came into the darkness of the demonic below.

- *Who met Jesus and his three disciples at the foot of the mountain, and what need did this person express (vv. 37–39)?*

- *To whom had this man already gone for help, and what were the results (v. 40)?*

- *How did Jesus respond to this (vv. 41–44)?*

- *What did the disciples still not understand (v. 45)?*

DIGGING DEEPER

Jesus' rebuke in verse 41 may have included the boy's father, but it covered more people than that. As New Testament scholar I. Howard Marshall comments: "Jesus' reply is apparently addressed to the father..., but it seems to refer to the people present generally, to the father who lacks faith in the power of God in the disciples, and to the disciples who lack faith in God to perform mighty works through themselves. They are members of an unbelieving generation."[63]

The disciples' lack of understanding about Jesus' imminent future also speaks to their lack of faith, but this time it was not faith as trust in Jesus but the insight of faith. They failed to grasp the fullness of Jesus' identity and mission. "The disciples were still confused as to how Jesus, with His glorious power, could experience a humiliating death. Nor could they put together the crowd's reaction to His miracles and His prediction that the nation would turn against Him and kill Him."[64]

Greatness Recast

Further evidence of their lack of understanding came when the disciples argued over "who would be the greatest one among them" (v. 46).

- *Jesus gave them a lesson that recast greatness and, thereby, discipleship. What was the lesson (vv. 47–48)?*

John then conveyed yet another failure to understand discipleship and mission.

- *What issue did John bring up to Jesus, and what was Jesus' response (vv. 49–50)?*

Recall that John, along with the other disciples, had already seen God's power working through them (v. 6), and yet he was one of the students of the group who had failed to cast out a demon from the father's son (v. 40). Nevertheless, he was willing to try to stop someone who was not of their group from doing God's work more effectively than they had.

• *Have you ever encountered believers who were so jealous of their positions of authority that they turned against other believers who were actually doing a better job than they were? Describe what occurred.*

• *What did you learn through this situation?*

Grasping Jesus' Mission

On yet another occasion, two of Jesus' disciples demonstrated their ongoing failure to grasp his mission.

• *Read verses 51–56. Summarize what happens and the clarity Jesus brings to his mission.*

• *Given what Jesus said, how would you restate what he had come to do?*

- *It's much easier to wish divine judgment on others than it is to seek to woo them to put their lives in Jesus' hands. One day, God's final judgment will come, but Jesus wanted his followers to put their focus and energy elsewhere. Where is your focus when it comes to those who oppose Christ and his teachings?*

The Cost of Discipleship

While traveling to Jerusalem, three different people approached Jesus and expressed a desire to follow him. He responded to each person, but Luke doesn't tell us what each person did as a result. We're left to consider how we would have responded to Jesus if we had been in each person's sandals.

I Will Follow You Wherever

- *What did the first person tell Jesus he wanted to do, and what did Jesus say in return (vv. 57–58)?*

- *Are you willing to sacrifice material blessings and securities to follow Jesus? Why or why not?*

I Will, but First, Family Duty

- *Jesus invited the second man to join him, but what did this person want to do first (v. 59)?*

- *What was Jesus' response (v. 60)?*

Bible commentator David Garland provides important insight on what Jesus said:

> "Leave the dead to bury their own dead" sounds extraordinarily harsh to someone in a time of grief. But the "dead" is a metaphorical reference to those who make no response to Jesus (see Eph 2:1, 5). The premise behind this command is that outside of the sphere of discipleship to Jesus there is only death. The spiritually dead can bury those who are physically dead. If the man postpones discipleship, he belongs to the living dead.[65]

- *Are you willing to forego even a family member's funeral if an opportunity for Christian ministry arises? Why or why not?*

I Will, but First, Goodbyes

- *What did the third individual say about his plans for following Jesus (Luke 9:61)?*

- *What did Jesus say to him (v. 62)?*

- *Are you allowing your past to negatively influence your ability to follow and obey Jesus? Why or why not?*

Getting the Work Done

Once again, Jesus gave his disciples a mission to accomplish, even though they had shown themselves to be still somewhat unprepared for it.

- *How many teams and disciples did Jesus organize (10:1)? What is the larger biblical significance of the total number (see study note 'b' for verse 1)?*

- *What were the basic to-do instructions he gave them (vv. 2–11)?*

- *What did Jesus tell them about the judgment that will come upon those communities that reject them (vv. 12–15)?*

- *What was his closing comment to them about the significance of their mission (v. 16)?*

- *How successful were the disciples in their mission (v. 17)?*

- *What conclusion did Jesus draw for them about their success (vv. 18–20)?*

- *Then Jesus broke out in a Spirit-inspired prayer that his disciples apparently heard. Summarize what Jesus said in his prayer (vv. 21–22).*

- *How privileged were the disciples to be with rabbi Jesus (vv. 23–24)?*

Neighbor Love

Luke records another incident that apparently occurred while Jesus was teaching. In his day, "Teachers sat, and students stood in courtesy."[66] Among those listening was a "religious scholar" (Luke 10:25). The original Greek text identifies this man as a lawyer. Jewish lawyers majored in the Mosaic law found in the first five books of the Hebrew Scriptures (Genesis through Deuteronomy, also known as the Torah). They also studied the rest of Scripture, especially as it related to the understanding and application of the Torah.

- *Did this expert in the law come to learn from Jesus or to do something else (v. 25)?*

- *Describe the first part of the exchange between this lawyer and Jesus (vv. 25–28).*

- *What did the lawyer ask next, and what does Luke say is the reason he asked that question (v. 29)?*

- *Summarize the story Jesus tells and the question he poses after it (vv. 30–36).*

- *How did the exchange end (v. 37)?*

- *Do you think that the lawyer got what he expected when he began his challenge of Jesus and his teachings? Support your answer.*

THE BACKSTORY

Jesus made the hero of his story a Samaritan. This would have been shocking, not only to the lawyer but also to every Jew who was within earshot. You see...

> Jews *hated* Samaritans. The Mishnah, a collection of written laws considered by many Jews to be second in authority only to the Hebrew Scriptures, declares, "He that eats the bread of the Samaritans is like to one that eats the flesh of swine."...
> The animosity between Jews and Samaritans was centuries old; they despised and often went out of their way

to avoid one another. To Jews, Samaritans were heretics (among other things). Samaritans accepted the five books of Moses as authoritative but rejected the rest of the Hebrew canon. Samaritans also believed in worshiping one God, but they held that Shechem (rather than Jerusalem) was the true site of worship.[67]

In the story, the Samaritan not only took care of the stranger's immediate physical needs but also put the injured man on his own mount, took him to an inn, and paid for the stranger's caretaking, with a promise to handle all future expenses related to his care. "The Samaritan's prescient settling of additional bills that might accumulate was important (vv. 34–35); stripped of his belongings, the stranger lacked the ability to pay, and if he could not pay, he would not be permitted to leave, perhaps even be arrested and thrown into debtor's prison."[68]

Now, after Jesus told this tough-to-handle story, he did not repeat the lawyer's question, "What do you mean by 'my neighbor'?" (v. 29). Instead, Jesus posed what he saw as the more important question: "Which one of the three men who saw the wounded man proved to be the true neighbor?" (v. 36).

To Jesus, the true question was, *What kind of neighbor must I be?* The real issue concerns the one who should love and the extent to which that love should be shown. Once that's settled, the answer to the first query is simple: *Everyone* is my neighbor, including my enemies! Authentic neighbor-love has no limits—not race, nationality, worldview, social status, physical condition, or any other factor. The uncompromising standard of love is that we love whoever crosses our path. This requires that we become lovers ourselves.[69]

❤ SHARE GOD'S HEART

- *Whom do you love? How far does your circle of love extend?*

- *Do you know someone who needs loving attention, loving care? If so, do you have the means to meet their need, even partially? Extend your love to this person in ways that will matter. Don't wait. Be a good Samaritan.*

The Better Choice

Still on their way to Jerusalem, Jesus and his disciples came into a village where they were invited by Martha into her home—a home she shared with her sister, Mary (vv. 38–39).

- *Describe what occurred while Jesus was there (vv. 38–42).*

- *In your own words, express why Jesus commended Mary's choice over Martha's.*

 EXPERIENCE GOD'S HEART

Repeatedly, Jesus urged his followers to listen to him, to understand his teaching, and *then* to put it into practice (see 6:46–49; 8:15, 17–18, 21; 9:6). In other words, first comes hearing, then comes doing.

- *Jesus' teaching is found in Scripture. Do you have a Bible study plan that allows you to pull away from other duties and distractions to truly focus on learning the Word of God? If so, what is your plan, and how regularly do you engage in it?*

- *If you don't have a Bible study plan, the fact that you are working through this study guide shows that you are at least open to one and have even begun one. One resource that has benefitted countless Christians is by Dr. Howard Hendricks and his son, William Hendricks. The book is titled Living by the Book: The Art and Science of Reading the Bible. You can also find numerous other printed and online sources to help you learn how to study God's Word and apply it well in your life.*

All about Prayer

While Jesus often went off alone to pray (Luke 5:16; 6:12; cf. Mark 1:35; Matthew 14:23), he also prayed with his followers near him. This was one of those occasions. One of his disciples, seeing that Jesus had just finished praying, asked him to teach them how to pray (Luke 11:1).

- *What was the model prayer Jesus gave them (Luke 11:2–4)?*

- *With whom does the prayer begin, and on what topic does it end?*

- *What do you find most significant in this prayer for your own prayer practice?*

After providing a model prayer, Jesus encouraged his followers to pray with persistence.

- *Summarize the story Jesus told (vv. 5–8).*

- *What point of application did he draw from his story (vv. 9–10)?*

- *From your own prayer experience, why do you think Jesus homed in on persistence? After all, he could have dealt with a number of other topics related to prayer, such as where to pray, issues worthy of prayer, length of prayer time, even one's physical position in prayer. Why, then, persistence?*

- *Next Jesus focused on what his followers could expect from the One they prayed to. What could they know the Father would provide for them? What did they know the Father would never give them (vv. 11–13)?*

- *Reflect on the Holy Spirit's role in the life and ministry of Jesus as Luke has presented it. Do you think the Spirit could play a similar role in your life? Why or why not?*

Talking It Out

1. Throughout Scripture, when God comes in glory, he reveals himself: "God's objective glory is revealed by his coming to be present with us, his people, and to show us himself by his actions in our world."[70] God was uniquely present in the incarnation of his Son, Jesus, but only those who had eyes to see recognized him for who he was (John 1). At the Transfiguration, a few of Jesus' disciples saw a fuller manifestation of his glory. Why do you think Jesus did not show his glory this way to all his followers?

2. Jesus' ministry and that of his disciples often included dealings with demons. Like his first-century followers, Jesus has given us authority to trample on Satan's kingdom, and we do this every time we choose to serve in his name, to give ourselves to hearing and obeying him rather than rebelling against him. Did you realize that your Christian life and service hits Satan right where it hurts? Do you understand that you are a warrior in a spiritual war that predates you and that Christ has already won? Share with one another what you know about this spiritual conflict and how Luke's Gospel helps you better understand it and your place in it.

3. Whom would you point to in your life who loves well? What distinguishes their expressions of love and to whom do they share their love? Does this person remind you of the good Samaritan Jesus talked about?

LESSON 7

Critics and Warnings

(11:14–13:17)

In a broken world, truth will foster enemies, and error will find friends. While some people want to know the truth, even many of them find reasons to reject certain truths that hit too close to the heart, too close to their protected self-perception, to their social or professional standing, to the image they have worked so hard to project.

During Jesus' ministry, he who was truth incarnate came face-to-face with people who found him threatening. His teaching was more profound than theirs, his power greater, his knowledge deeper and wiser, his compassion more extensive, his popularity a rival. When they looked at Jesus, they saw a man they needed to put down. He had to be neutralized at least—even better, demonized and rejected. The people had to see him as he "really" was—a man who used Satan's power, not God's, who violated Scripture, not upheld and obeyed it. Jesus had to go. But how?

In this section of Luke's Gospel, we see Jesus encountering stiffened resistance to him, his message, and his actions. We also see how Jesus battled unjust criticism and the critics who launched it.

Light vs. Darkness

- *Luke records another miracle Jesus performed. What was it, and how did most of the people respond to it (11:14)?*

- *Some people in the crowd criticized Jesus.*

  One group claimed (v. 15)...

  Another group claimed (v. 16)...

- *What was Jesus' response to the first group (vv. 17–28)?*

- *What was his response to the second group (vv. 29–32)?*

- *Then Jesus addressed comments to both sets of critics, and he likely had the rest of the crowd in mind too. Summarize what he said (vv. 33–36).*

- *Now compare Jesus' comments, especially those about the heart and receiving revelation, to his earlier parable about the soil and the seed (8:11–15). What kind of heart/soil did his critics in this crowd unveil about themselves?*

Religious Hypocrisy Exposed

Next we find Jesus was invited into the home of a Pharisee, and his host had invited other religious leaders as well (11:37–38). We quickly learn that Jesus was among people who were watching his every move and had expectations of what counted toward righteousness and what did not.

- *What did the host immediately notice about Jesus that shocked him (vv. 37–38)?*

The text doesn't tell us if the Pharisee said anything to Jesus, but Jesus clearly saw the reaction of this religious leader to Jesus' failure to wash his hands. As Morris explains, for the Pharisees, washing one's hands "had nothing to do with hygiene but was a rule made in the interests of ceremonial purity." Continuing, Morris says:

> Before eating anything, scrupulous Jews had water poured over their hands to remove the defilement contracted by their contact with a sinful world. The quantity of water and the manner of washing are prescribed in minute detail in the Mishnah (*Yadaim* 1:1ff.). The Pharisee clearly expected that Jesus, as a noted religious teacher, would conform to the accepted practice.[71]

- *Jesus' response exposed the false religiosity of the Pharisees. Read what he said in Luke 11:39–44 and then answer the following questions.*

  What was Jesus' overall charge against the Pharisees?

  What evidence did he provide that his charge was accurate?

  What did Jesus say that the Pharisees should have been doing instead?

- *The religious lawyers then spoke up and said what to Jesus (v. 45)?*

- *Read verses 46–52, then answer the questions that follow.*

  What was Jesus' overall charge against these experts in interpreting Scripture?

What evidence did he provide in support of his charge?

What did Jesus say that God would do in response to such abuse of his Word?

• *What was the fallout that came upon Jesus for his comments and criticisms (vv. 53–54)?*

These religious leaders went after Jesus, trying to discredit him with as many verbal weapons as they had so they could preserve their now tattered reputations.

Religious hypocrisy is still alive and well. As Garland writes:

> Religious people of all stripes can easily
> fool themselves into believing that their
> exhaustive religiosity covers their sins.
> Jesus' attack on these representative
> religious leaders for their moral turpitude
> that strips all of their religiosity of any
> meaning is an attack on all who seek honor
> for themselves, wear public masks of piety,
> and expect adoration. They are no less
> guilty of intellectual duplicity and moral
> corruption. They hide behind the power of
> their religious authority that permits them
> to continue their abuse with impunity.[72]

- *Do you seek honor for yourself? Or do you wear a public mask of piety? Or do you attempt to cover over internal sin through outward religious observances? Ask God to show you your inner self, to reveal what's really going on inside you. Then repent of any exposed sin and ask him to empower you to live more humbly before him and more faithfully to him.*

Jesus then took the opportunity to warn his disciples about religious hypocrisy and persecution and how to face them.

- *In warning his disciples "of the hypocrisy of the Pharisees," Jesus first focused on the hypocrites and then turned to his followers to pass along truth and counsel.*

   What did Jesus say about the Pharisees (12:1–2)?

   What truths and applications did he pass along to his followers (vv. 3–12)?

Putting God First...

Now that Jesus had addressed religious hypocrisy, two matters came up that had to do with putting God first.

Over Material Possessions

- *Someone from the crowd spoke up and called on Jesus to side with him. What demand did he make on the Lord (v. 13)?*

- *What was Jesus' initial response (v. 14; see study note 'a' on this verse)?*

- *What did Jesus imply was the focus of the question from the crowd, and how did he address that central point (vv. 15–21)?*

- *What is your attitude and practice toward material possessions, especially in relationship to God?*

Over Daily Needs and Worry

- *Building on what he had said, Jesus shifted gears a bit and spoke to a related matter. What primary subject did he address next, and how did he want his hearers to respond to it (vv. 22–32)?*

- *Jesus then drew a concluding application for his disciples. What was it (vv. 33–34)?*

9 SHARE GOD'S HEART

Jesus didn't want material goods to possess his followers. Instead, he wanted them to use their material possessions to help those who needed them more. In the process, they would be putting their confidence in God to meet their own needs and enriching their heavenly account by imitating the generosity of the Lord. Or, as Garland puts it, "The truth is that greater happiness derives from the experience of sharing things with others than from miserly attempts to accumulate and to stash them away."[73]

- *Have you ever used your material possessions to bring good to someone in need? If so, tell the story.*

- *Consider an individual, a family, a charity, or a situation that presents a need and determine how you can help out by using what you have. God has blessed you to be a blessing to others, not to hold tightly to what you have received. Keep a heavenly perspective. In that way, you will be of more earthly good.*

Preparation for the Second Coming

Jesus then turned his instruction to telling his disciples how to behave until his return. Jesus already had one coming: his miraculous conception and birth. His second coming is yet to occur, and that was his focus in this section of Luke's Gospel.

- *How prepared for his return does Jesus expect his followers to be (v. 35)?*

- *To what did Jesus compare the kind of anticipation the disciples should have for his return (vv. 36–40)?*

- *What question did Peter then ask of Jesus (v. 41)?*

- *Jesus compares his followers to the behavior of servants when the master is away. Explain this comparison. How does it relate to Christians today (vv. 42–48)?*

Division and Discernment

Jesus then turned from his second coming toward his first coming.

- *What did Jesus come to do, and how would his time here "change everything" (vv. 49–53)?*

- *We don't often consider that Jesus is a controversial, divisive figure. He was in his day, and he still is in ours. Have you experienced this aspect of Jesus and his message? If so, what has that been like for you?*

- *Why is Jesus often a divisive figure?*

- *If Jesus brought division at times, do you think you will, too, as one of his followers? Support your answer.*

- *Jesus addressed the crowds who had been listening in to the teaching he gave to his followers. Read verses 54–57 and summarize Jesus' message.*

- *How good are you at discerning the spiritual significance of the times in which you live?*

Jesus wrapped up his comments on discerning the times with a reference to a court of law (vv. 58–59). He uses this illustration "to drive home the point that people need to be rightly related to God. Even in the earthly sphere it makes sense to try hard to be reconciled with an opponent—even on the way...to the magistrate—in order to avoid being thrown into prison and having to pay the last penny. How much more important it is to 'be reconciled' when the opponent is God!"[74]

The Time for Repentance

Then some individuals in the crowd "informed Jesus that Pilate had slaughtered some Galilean Jews while they were offering sacrifices at the temple, mixing their blood with the sacrifices they were offering" (13:1).

During this time in Jesus' ministry, Pontius Pilate was the prefect, or governor, of Judea. The Roman emperor Tiberius (AD 14–37) appointed Pilate to this post in the year 26, and he served in that position until year 36. He had "the second-longest tenure of any first-century Roman governor in Palestine." Tiberius, an able administrator himself, insisted on having good administrators serving in important roles under him. Given the length of time Pilate served, there's good reason to believe that he had the approval of Tiberius. That said, Pilate found "the governorship of Judea a most taxing experience."[75] He was involved in several incidents that provoked severe criticism and even demonstrations from his subjects. The one mentioned here in Luke about the Galileans provides all the information we have on it, while the writings of the ancient historians Josephus and Philo mention the others.

- *What did Jesus tell the crowd about the slaughter of the Galilean Jews (13:2–3)?*

It was a common belief among first-century Jews that when calamity struck, it was punishment for human sin, and the greater the tragedy, the greater the sin (see John 9:1–2; cf. Job 4:7–9; 22:4–11). Luke doesn't specify why some in the crowd brought the Galilean massacre to Jesus' attention, but he does tell us that Jesus used the incident to draw attention to the crowd's need to repent of *their* sins lest judgment come upon them too.

- *Jesus brought up a different incident. What was it, and what point did Jesus make regarding it (Luke 13:4–5)?*

- *To drive home his point and even add to it, Jesus told a parable (vv. 6–9). Summarize the story.*

Although Jesus didn't specify repentance in the story, the theme undergirds it, and to it, he added the need to bear fruit. In other words, the truly repentant will produce spiritual/moral fruit; their deeds will match their profession of faith. Of course, it may take time for a changed person to begin to produce the requisite fruit. God grants time; he is gracious after all. However, he also knows when the lack of fruit-bearing reveals a heart that is not as repentant as the person's words allege. In those cases, God's judgment will come.

Sabbath Healing

Once again in this chapter of Luke, we find Jesus teaching in a synagogue.

- *Who approached him while he was teaching? What was her condition, and what did Jesus do to help her (vv. 10–13)?*

- *How did the ruler of this synagogue react to what Jesus did (v. 14)?*

- *Read verses 15–16 and summarize Jesus' response to this man.*

- *What was the significance of Jesus calling the now healed woman a "beloved daughter of Abraham" (v. 16; see study note 'c')?*

- *What was the result of Jesus' rebuttal (v. 17)?*

THE BACKSTORY

Morris explains that a ruler of the synagogue was an "official who was responsible for the arrangements at the synagogue services. He would select, for example, those who would lead in prayer, read the Scripture and preach. He was thus a man of eminence in the community."[76] That such a religious leader would angrily challenge Jesus for healing on the Sabbath was an official indictment against what Jesus did. And yet, rather than backing down, Jesus charged the man with hypocrisy and with exalting the value of animal life and care over that of human life and care.

- *Do you see human life as more valuable than animal life? Support your answer, especially from Scripture.*

EXPERIENCE GOD'S HEART

Luke repeatedly brings out the fact that Jesus confronted his critics and did so effectively. Jesus used Scripture, reason, story, history, and human experience to clarify his teaching, to explain his actions, and to refute his critics' claims and arguments.

- *Do you stand up for what you believe? Why or why not?*

- *Do you know why you believe what you believe? Why or why not?*

- *Are you willing to follow the Lord's example to defend what you know is true? Why or why not?*

Talking It Out

1. Who or what is first in your life? God? Career? School? Friends? Parents? Church? What evidence could people point to that would verify what/who you say is number one in your life?

2. How would you describe the times in which we now live? What do they tell you about the spiritual condition of your culture, your country, and your church?

3. Jesus repeatedly couples acts of service with teaching the truth. What are some ways you can serve others while also being a spokesperson for the truth?

LESSON 8

Lost and Found

(13:18–16:31)

Jesus was a consummate storyteller. His stories were never too long; in fact, many were short. And he never named the characters in his stories—well, almost never. In one story, one of the characters had a name, and the story comes up in this lesson. One thing is for sure: Jesus' stories were never wasted. They centered on truth. Sometimes his hearers missed the story's truth but not always. Even when they grasped the story's point, they didn't always welcome it. Still, Jesus' stories have been retold in countless ways since he first uttered them. And they are so familiar that sometimes we miss their power.

Let's see if we can recapture these stories and allow them to penetrate us anew.

God's Kingdom

After healing the woman at the synagogue on the Sabbath, Jesus told two stories, both of which were intended to describe the kingdom of God through ordinary activities. These stories are analogies, using the ordinary to describe the extraordinary, the natural to depict the supernatural. They both start with the same idea: "God's kingdom is like…"

- *To what did Jesus compare God's kingdom in his first story (Luke 13:18–19)?*

- *What was the meaning of this story (see study note 'd' for verse 19)?*

- *To what did Jesus compare God's kingdom in his second story (vv. 20–21)?*

- *What does this story tell us about God's kingdom (see study note 'e' for verse 21)?*

- *Combined, what insight do these stories give you about God's kingdom and how it grows and influences?*

- *While Jesus was still on the road, a bystander asked him how many will be saved to eternal life (vv. 22–23). Rather than answer the person's question, Jesus focused on what matters more. Read verses 24–30. Summarize what Jesus chose to talk about and why it would be more important than learning how many will be saved.*

- *Some Jews believed that just because they were Jews, God favored them for eternal life. Imagine them hearing Jesus' answer. How do you think they might have reacted to what Jesus said?*

Herod Antipas and Jerusalem

Now some religious leaders, in this case Pharisees, warned Jesus about Herod Antipas's intent to kill him (v. 31). Luke doesn't say if the motive of these Pharisees was genuine or not. He is more interested in letting his readers know how Jesus responded to them.

- *Read what Jesus says in verses 32–35, and then answer the following questions.*

    Did Jesus seem concerned about Herod Antipas's intentions? Why or why not?

What was Jesus' depiction of Jerusalem?

What did Jesus predict would happen to this city?

A Sabbath Healing

Jesus had healed on the Sabbath three times already (4:31–37; 6:6–11; 13:10–17). This time, it happened while he was on his way to dine with some Pharisees and religious lawyers (14:1–6).

• *Read 14:1–6 and describe what happened.*

• *Rather than being amazed by the miracle and giving God glory for it, how did the religious leaders react? Why do you think they chose to respond this way?*

Humility, Hospitality, and Discipleship

While still at the same Pharisee's house, Jesus noticed "the guests jockeying to grab the seats closest to the host that will bestow on them the badge of highest ranking in the social pecking order" (see 14:7).[77]

- *What warning did Jesus give about such behavior (vv. 8–11)?*

- *Jesus then turned to his host. What advice did he give this man (vv. 12–14)?*

- *One dinner guest picked up on Jesus' reference to the future "resurrection of the godly" (v. 14). What did the guest believe about this future event (v. 15)?*

- *Jesus responded to him with a parable. Read verses 16–24, and then answer the following questions.*

  At the time he was speaking, Jesus was in the home of an elite religious leader who was hosting a feast for other religious leaders. Why do you imagine Jesus told a story about a feast where those initially invited make excuses and don't attend?

  Who, then, was finally invited and actually went to the feast in the story? Were any of the guests among the social or religious elite?

Jesus' punchline to the story comes in verse 24. What is it? What message did it send to those religious leaders who were dining with him at that moment?

The Cost of Discipleship

Luke takes us away from the dining room and back out into the byways where "massive crowds" were again following Jesus (v. 25). When Jesus spoke to them, his theme was discipleship, but this time he urged them to count the cost before committing to him.

- *Read verses 25–35. Consult study note 'a' for verse 26 as well. What was Jesus' teaching about the cost of discipleship?*

 EXPERIENCE GOD'S HEART

- *Did you count the cost of following Jesus before you made a commitment to him? Many people don't. Have you done so since you first put your faith in him? If not, you can now. What has it cost you to follow him so far?*

- *What do you imagine the cost might be to remain committed to Jesus?*

- *Is the cost worth it? Why or why not?*

Parables of the Lost

Among those who listened to Jesus were certain undesirable individuals, which upset the sensibilities of "Jewish religious leaders and experts of the law" (15:2).

- *What problem did the religious leaders and lawyers express about the people Jesus attracted (15:1–2)?*

Jesus, undeterred by the criticism, presented three stories that focused on the lost, their inherent worth, and the heavenly joy that comes when any of them repent.

- *Read the parable of the lost lamb and summarize it below, including the conclusion Jesus drew from it (vv. 4–7).*

- *Consider now the parable of the lost coin and the main point Jesus made about it, summarizing all of this below (vv. 8–10).*

- *The final story Jesus told was about two sons—one who leaves and returns and the other who stays but refuses to celebrate when his brother comes home (vv. 11–32). Read the story, noting especially the actions of the two sons and how their father deals with each of them. Then answer the questions that follow.*

> *Which son was lost and repented? How did his father treat him?*

> *Which son stayed home but refused to rejoice over the return of his lost brother? How did his father treat him?*

> *Among the Jews and gentiles who listened to Jesus, which ones would you say more closely resembled the prodigal son who returned? Why?*

> *Which would you say more closely resembled the son who stayed home? Why?*

In the parable, the human father symbolizes God the Father. What do you learn about how God regards us, whether we stray away from home or remain close but lack a godly perspective and attitude?

❤ SHARE GOD'S HEART

Since "both Jews and gentiles are all under the bondage of sin" (Romans 3:9), as the apostle Paul concludes, all of us can find ourselves in Jesus' story of the wayward sons. While the son who left home and squandered his inheritance is the more obvious prodigal, the son who stayed home was also lost. When the younger son asked for his "share" of his father's estate, in effect, he was declaring to his father, "I wish you were already dead!"[78] The older son was in the room when his brother demanded his inheritance, and the father "went ahead and distributed between *the two sons their inheritance*" (Luke 15:12, emphasis added). The older son did not dispute what his younger sibling said to their father. He didn't defend his father. Instead, he silently acquiesced and accepted his share of the inheritance too. While the older son didn't blatantly disparage their father, his actions betrayed that he was just as disloyal and coldhearted toward their father as his brother.

Still, the father treated both sons the same. He divided the inheritance between his sons and let them do with it as they wished. He didn't rebuke either one. His generosity and love extended to them both.

It was not until the younger son returned to his father repentant and his father responded with such an extravagant expression of forgiveness and celebration that the older son's mask dropped away more fully. "Suddenly, there becomes glaringly visible a resentful, proud, unkind, selfish person, one that had remained deeply hidden."[79] This son unleashes his vitriol on his father—and still, the father responds with abiding love and compassion for both sons.

What Jesus doesn't reveal is whether the older son repents as his younger brother had done. Jesus' parable leaves us with one son's response still lingering. Will he come "home" too? Remember, the father has to leave the house to go out to the older son (v. 28). Will this son come into the house? Will he join the celebration by recognizing his own sin, repenting of it, and changing his response to grace and love?

- *You may know someone who is more like the older son than the younger one. Or perhaps the prodigal you know resembles the younger son more. Whichever is the case, take some time right now to pray for this person and their situation and condition of heart. Ask God the Father, through the work of his Spirit, to soften this person's heart toward divine love and grace. Then, as the opportunity arises, prepare yourself, like the father in the parable, to offer our heavenly Father's compassion to this prodigal. You may not need to do this in words, but it can and should always come in your actions toward others.*

Kingdom Life

The next story Jesus told was directed to his disciples (Luke 16:1). Then, an interruption by some greedy "Jewish religious leaders" (v. 14) led him to tell the only story in which he names one of the characters.

Managing Well

- *Read Luke 16:1–8. Summarize the story, especially including the manager's motives for his actions.*

- *Would you say that either the rich businessman or his manager has a virtuous character? Provide some support for your answer.*

- *Were those in debt behaving any better? Why or why not?*

- *Why would Jesus use a story with such unsavory characters? See what he says in verses 8–9 for help answering this question.*

- *At first, Jesus drew a concluding lesson from the story by focusing on generosity and eternal reward (v. 9). Then he drew from it a different lesson with a different focus. To what subject did he change, and what lesson did he bring out of it (vv. 10–13)?*

Loyalties and Love

The Jewish religious leaders who heard Jesus' story couldn't contain themselves. They mocked his teaching.

- *Why did they laugh at Jesus (v. 14)?*

- *How did Jesus answer them (v. 15)?*

- *What had they missed in God's Word and in his activity in their own day because of their love of the wrong things and their practices and teachings that actually undermined God's Word (vv. 13, 16–18)?*

- *Jesus then told another story with the religious leaders listening in. In this story, a character was named Lazarus. And he was anything but wealthy. Read verses 19–31 and answer the questions that follow.*

  What were the earthly living conditions of the story's two main characters?

  After death, where did each person end up?

What was the condition of each man in the afterlife?

What did the rich man want for his still living relatives, and why did Father Abraham deny his request?

How was this story an indictment against the religious leaders because of what they loved over God and how they disregarded God's Word?

Talking It Out

1. Jesus' kingdom parables (13:18–22) emphasize how small the kingdom begins and how expansive it becomes. Discuss what you know about ministries inside or outside of your church, especially how they have grown. How small was their start? How large have they become? What is their potential for future growth? Do you find all this encouraging? If so, explain your answer.

2. In various ways, Jesus' life and teaching demonstrate the wide variety of people invited to be part of God's everlasting kingdom. In this lesson, what did you learn about God's acceptance of human beings? Does our ethnicity, economic or social status, religious or political position, career choice, or anything similar seem to qualify us for or disqualify us from his love, forgiveness, and gift of everlasting life? Support your answer.

3. Jesus' story about Lazarus provides a glimpse into the afterlife (16:19–31). What did you learn about that life? What would you conclude from the story about who is destined for heaven over hell? Can we always tell from the way a person looks and lives which future is in store for them? Explain your answer.

LESSON 9

Kingdom Life

(17:1–19:27)

Before Jesus arrived in the religious and political center of Israel, his days were filled with more teaching than healing. He still had much to say, especially to his students. And as he had done throughout his ministry, he ensured that his actions fit his words. Just as he knew that God's wisdom would "be proven true by the expressions of godliness in everyone who follows me" (Luke 7:35), he who was wisdom incarnate—he who had been empowered and led his entire life by God's Spirit—continued to impart wisdom, knowing that only those who had ears to hear and eyes to see would truly grasp it.

Let's return to Luke's marvelous narrative to learn what Jesus had to say as he moved ever closer to the death that awaited him in Jerusalem.

Forgiveness, Faith, and Obedience

The subject of forgiveness came up in connection to something Jesus knew he would face in Jerusalem.

- *Jesus began with the subject of betrayals. What did he say about those who betray others? (17:1–2)?*

- *Later Jesus would tell his disciples what awaited him in Jerusalem. What was that (18:32–33), and how did it relate to what he said about the matter in the first part of chapter 17?*

- *After bringing up his main subject, Jesus drew an application for his followers. What was it, and how did his disciples react to it (17:2–5)?*

- *The apostles wanted more faith. How did Jesus correct their understanding about faith (v. 6; see also study note 'g' for this verse)?*

- *Along with changing their view of faith, what attitude did Jesus say they should have while exercising their faith (vv. 7–10)?*

Gratitude

While Jesus was still on the road to Jerusalem, ten men with leprosy came within shouting distance of him (vv. 11–12).

- *What did the men call out to Jesus, and how did he respond (vv. 13–14)?*

- *What did Jesus do for the men with leprosy, and what was their response (vv. 14–18)?*

- *What were Jesus' final words to the Samaritan man healed of leprosy who showed such gratitude toward Jesus and insight about who Jesus was (v. 19)?*

DIGGING DEEPER

In Luke's account, Jesus looked at these men with leprosy and spoke to them, even though society treated them as outcasts. Still, he did not go to them or touch them. As Morris points out:

> He did not even say, 'You are cured!' He told them, leprous as they were, to go and show themselves to the priests, the normal procedure when a leper was cured. The priest acted as a kind of health inspector to

certify that the cure had in fact taken place (Lev. 14:2ff.). Jesus was putting their faith to the test by asking these men to act as though they had been cured. And as they obeyed so it happened: *as they went they were cleansed.*[80]

But only one of the cured men demonstrated gratitude to Jesus, and he also showed insight into Jesus' identity as the Messiah. And this cured man was a Samaritan, not a Jew. Unlike so many of the Jewish religious leaders who were hostile to Jesus and tried to do all they could to silence and marginalize him, a man outside of Jewish orthodoxy, one who had been ostracized from Jewish and even Samaritan society, saw Jesus as the long-anticipated Savior. This healed Samaritan "has faith and responds faithfully to the mercy he has received. It is on this basis, and not because of his status as a Jew—measured either by physical ancestry and/or by ritual purity—that he receives salvation."[81]

God's Kingdom and Judgment

Some Jewish religious leaders asked Jesus "When will God's kingdom come?" (Luke 17:20). Jesus' response must have been a surprise.

• *What did he say to them (vv. 20–21; see also study note 'g')?*

• *How does his response compare to his earlier kingdom parables (see 13:18–21)?*

- *When Jesus was alone with his apostles, he spoke about the future side of God's kingdom, which involved his second coming. Read 17:22–37. Summarize what Jesus told them about what was yet to come.*

- *How do you feel when you read Jesus' end-times description? Are you ready for his second coming?*

Persistence and Humility

The next lengthier teaching time with his disciples was a focus on prayer—specifically, the exercise of persistence and humility while engaging God (18:1–17).

Persistent Engagement

- *Regarding praying persistently, Jesus began with a story and drew his application from it (18:1–8). Summarize the story and Jesus' follow-up instruction.*

DIGGING DEEPER

When Jesus says that God "will not delay" to answer the prayers of those believers who persist and that God will "give swift justice to those who don't give up" (vv. 7–8), we should not interpret those words as indicating immediacy on a human timetable. In Luke 17, Jesus talked about his second coming and the longing his followers would have for his return. He uttered those words about two thousand years ago. Indeed, we have been in the last days of human history as we know it since the first coming of Christ and the early church (see Hebrews 1:2; 1 John 2:18). And, as the apostle Peter noted, to an eternal God, "a thousand years counts as one day." So "contrary to man's perspective, the Lord is not late with his promise to return, as some measure lateness. But rather, his 'delay' simply reveals his loving patience toward you, because he does not want any to perish but all to come to repentance" (2 Peter 3:8–9). This is why persistence in prayer is so important. We must not lose hope when God's answer does not come within our timetable or look as we might expect.

When Jesus ended this part of his instruction, he shifted the discussion from what God will do to what Jesus will find upon his return to earth. Will he find people trusting in God as exhibited through persistent prayer? Or will their hope have waned and their prayers with it (Luke 18:8)?

EXPERIENCE GOD'S HEART

- *Have you sometimes found it difficult to persist in prayer? If so, why? If not, what has sustained your effort?*

- *What prayer request have you made that God has not yet answered? If you know it is something God would surely want to grant you, how about making a commitment to keep praying for it until his answer comes? And if you are unsure whether it is something God would say yes to, how about praying for it but also asking God to let you know if you should stop making the request? In other words, pray persistently and leave it in God's hands to tell you in his way if it's a request you should drop.*

Humble Engagement

- *The next topic Jesus addressed is humility—humility overall and humility in prayer. And again, he started with a story (Luke 18:9–13). Summarize it below.*

- *What life lesson did Jesus derive from the story (v. 14)?*

- *When people brought their children to Jesus and his disciples tried to discourage this, Jesus used the occasion to teach all of them another life lesson (vv. 15–17). What was that lesson?*

- *What would you say Jesus' lesson tells us about how we should receive not only the youngest among us but also the divine revelation that comes to us? Should we do so pridefully, disdainfully, humbly, graciously, spitefully...? What would you say?*

Commitment and Omnipotence

During one of Jesus' days of ministry, he was approached by a "wealthy Jewish nobleman of high standing" (v. 18). This man of elite social standing asked Jesus a question that led Jesus to reference the omnipotence of God.

- *What question did the man ask Jesus (v. 18)?*

- *Jesus first responded to the way the questioner addressed him. What did Jesus say about the title the man used (v. 19; see study note 'a' on this verse)?*

- *Then Jesus responded directly to the man's question. Read the exchange and summarize it below (vv. 20–25; see also study note 'b').*

- *What concern did those who heard the exchange raise (v. 26)?*

- *How did Jesus respond, including to Peter's follow-up comment (vv. 27–30)?*

ⓒ DIGGING DEEPER

The theological term *omnipotence* refers to God as all-powerful. His power is unlimited, unconstrained by the limits upon the power his creatures can exercise, whether they be angels, human beings, or animals. As theologian Norman Geisler writes, "'omnipotent' means that God can do whatever is possible to do… His power is unlimited and uninhibited by anything else."[82]

The only thing God cannot do is contradict who and what he is (2 Timothy 2:13). For example, because he is all-good, God cannot do evil (Psalm 5:4–6; 145:17; Isaiah 5:20; Habakkuk 1:13; Malachi 2:17; James 1:13–14, 17). Because God is inherently truthful, he cannot lie (Numbers 23:19; John 8:44–45; 14:6; Titus 1:2; Hebrews 6:18). Because God is essentially immortal, he cannot die or be corrupted or diminished in any way (Acts 17:24–25; Romans 1:23; 1 Timothy 1:17; 6:16).[83] And because he is all-knowing (omniscient), he cannot be deceived (Psalm 33:13–15; 139:1–6; Hebrews 4:13). God cannot do what is impossible for him, but he can do what is "humanly impossible" (Luke 18:27).

The Mystery of What's to Come

Once again, Jesus "took the Twelve aside" and spoke to them in private (Luke 18:31).

- *What did Jesus tell them (vv. 31–33)?*

- *Was this the first time Jesus had said these things to his followers? If not, when else had he told them about these events to come?*

- *Did the disciples understand what Jesus told them (v. 34)? Why or why not?*

- *Have you ever failed to grasp what God has revealed? If so, what was that like for you? How did you handle it?*

Sight to the Blind

In the city of Jericho, "a blind beggar" gained an audience with Jesus.

- *Read verses 35–43. Describe what happened between the blind beggar and Jesus.*

- *Have you ever experienced God opening your eyes to his reality or to his presence or to some aspect of his revelation? Describe what happened and how it changed you and your relationship with him.*

What Repentance Looks Like

Next Luke records an encounter Jesus had with a despised supervisor of tax collectors, a man named Zacchaeus (19:1–2).

- *How eager was Zacchaeus to meet Jesus (vv. 3–4)?*

- *What did Jesus say to him, and how did some in the crowd regard Jesus' decision (vv. 5–7)?*

- *How did Zacchaeus show his gratitude to Jesus, and what did Jesus tell him (vv. 8–10)?*

💙 SHARE GOD'S HEART

Zacchaeus demonstrates what genuine repentance looks like. It goes beyond saying "I'm sorry," and it includes acts that demonstrate a true change of heart.

- *Is there anything that you need to take to God in repentance? If so, do that now.*

- *If your repentance was over something that involved hurting another person, group, or even organization, what can you do for them that would show a genuine change of heart—a renewed commitment to love God first and others second?*

Contrasting Kings

This next section of Luke 19 contains a story Jesus told as he and his disciples were nearing Jerusalem, the place where Jesus would be betrayed, arrested, tried, and brutally executed—all before he rose from the grave. Up to this point in his ministry, many people had concluded that Jesus was the long-awaited Messiah who was to come and take his rightful throne and overthrow the Jews' Roman gentile overlords. The people were expecting a military conquest led by the king-to-be, Jesus. As F. F. Bruce says:

> No single form of messianic expectation was cherished by Jesus' contemporaries, but the hope of a military Messiah predominated. The promises of a prince of the house of David who would break the oppressor's yoke from his people's neck seemed to many to be designed for such a time as theirs, whether the yoke was imposed by a Herodian ruler or by a Roman governor.[84]

So the majority of the people were "convinced that God's kingdom would fully manifest when Jesus established it in Jerusalem" (Luke 19:11).

Jesus, however, knew that this was not why he had come. While he was the predicted Messiah, he did not have a kingdom that would be established through military might; instead, his kingdom was already present, growing as seed matures into a tree or as yeast generates within dough and turns into bread (13:18–21). It is a kingdom that grows within a person (17:21), so it spans beyond geographical and national boundaries. Moreover, while his kingdom brings division at times in families and between friends (12:51–53), it also ushers its citizens into a new spiritual family (8:21). As the Messiah-King, Jesus didn't come to kill but to give life and to even sacrifice his life for others. He came to forgive, not to exact vengeance. He came to heal, not to destroy. In other words, Jesus knew that what most people expected from him would not occur.

So how could he change their perspective (19:12)? He told them a story that served as a contrast to what he had been doing and teaching. The story fit best with what the people already knew to be the typical way of kings. And by telling it, Jesus allowed them to compare the character in the story to the man who was telling it. Was Jesus like the noble prince turned king in the story? Had he been treating people the way this king had? Had he presented the way of life that the king lived? The people had to decide for themselves.

- *Read Jesus' story in Luke 19:12–27 and then respond to the questions that follow:*

    Did Jesus come into the world as a "wealthy prince"? How did he arrive?

    Did Jesus go into a "distant land" where he secured his kingship? Where has he gone, and what has he done?

    Did Jesus have servants who carried out his business dealings? Whom did Jesus choose, and what relationship did they have with him?

    Did Jesus give his disciples money to invest? If not, what had he given them to do thus far?

What are the character qualities of the noble prince turned king in the story? Now compare and contrast this story's main character with Jesus. Would you say that the two individuals are more dissimilar than similar or vice versa?

The king eventually takes retribution on his enemies. From what you know about Jesus' end, did he take action against his enemies? (If you are not sure, read Luke 23:34.)

Commenting upon this parable, Bible scholar David Garland writes:

> The parable prepares for a contrast between the rulers of this world and Jesus, who is poised to enter Jerusalem as a king.
> God's reign does not mirror the way worldly kingdoms operate. They depend on political infighting, military power, and the annihilation of enemies…It is the way of the kings of this world to go to war against other kings (14:31–32) and to seek more status, more power, more land, and more taxes…
> …[But Jesus'] kingship is built on the sovereignty of the truth. His destiny is to give his life for others rather than to annihilate them.[85]

At his second coming, Jesus will come as judge and will vanquish his enemies (Revelation 19–20). But his first coming was a mission of mercy and grace, seeking to secure salvation for as many as will accept it. As Paul put it: "our Savior-God…longs for everyone to embrace his life and return to the full knowledge of the truth. For God is one, and there is one Mediator between God and the sons of men—the true man, Jesus, the Anointed One. He gave himself as ransom-payment for everyone. Now is the proper time for God to give the world this witness" (1 Timothy 2:3–6). In Luke's Gospel, we haven't yet come upon the "ransom-payment" Jesus will make. But unlike the king in his story, who was "strict," "impossible to please," and sought to exact gain from the efforts of others, Jesus lovingly sacrificed his life for even those who despise him so they might have a way to receive the greatest gift of all—everlasting life.

Jesus' kingship is far better than any other form of rule that this world has to offer.

Talking It Out

1. While Jesus showed mercy even to those who turned out to be ungrateful, it was the immense gratitude shown by the Samaritan man with leprosy that struck him the most and led him to grant him the fullness of salvation (Luke 17:16–19). God is merciful, even to the ungrateful, but salvation and the fullness of its healing, transformative power are granted only to the grateful. Why is this so?

2. Jesus honored children, and he called on his disciples to do the same, even to receive divine revelation as trustingly as children do (18:15–17). How do you regard children? How trusting are you that what you read in Scripture is true and reliable? Can you go to God with childlike openness? Or do you approach him as if you were his judge?

3. Jesus told the wealthy nobleman, "It is next to impossible for those who have everything to enter into God's kingdom" (18:24). Why is this so? And what can break the power that possessions tend to wield?

LESSON 10

The King in the City

(19:28–21:38)

The first confirmed mention in history of the city that would later become known as Jerusalem comes from Egypt (ca. 1900–1800 BC). At that time, the city was named *Rushalimum*, a Canaanite name. The city is first mentioned in Scripture in Genesis 14:18, when a king-priest named Melchizedek meets up with Abraham. Melchizedek was "the king of Salem"—a city-state that sat on the same site as Jerusalem. *Salem* was the Canaanite term for "peace." It "would later give rise to the very meaningful Hebrew greeting *Shalom*,"[86] and Salem would give its five letters to the later and longer city name, Jeru*salem*, which means "place of peace."[87]

The city, however, had rarely known peace, especially in Jesus' day. "Conflict was constant between Jewish residents and Roman occupants in Jerusalem; between Jewish nationalists and loyalists to the foreign-based government. A war of words and ideas often escalated into episodes of deadly violence."[88]

Around and throughout the city were various walls, one of which included sixty towers. "Even Jewish worship in Jerusalem took place behind walls."[89]

The city bustled with commerce because major trade routes intersected in the city. It also had many government buildings and even a fort of Roman soldiers. All of this indicated that it was a cosmopolitan city and a populous one at that. Rome's Tenth Legion was stationed in Jerusalem, and it was almost ten thousand people strong—a number that included soldiers and support personnel. This Roman legion maintained order in the Judean province and posed a threat to possible rioters, especially during the times of religious festivals. "During these religious celebrations, it is estimated that 80,000–100,000 worshipers poured into Jerusalem. When you add this to the already 150,000–200,000 population at the time of Christ, there could be almost a quarter of a million people trying to witness the ceremonies at the temple courts."[90]

Jerusalem was also incredibly beautiful.

> Wealthy residents had built impressive palaces there. A six-thousand-square-foot mansion overlooked the temple area. Many ancient monuments in Jerusalem reflected architectural genius. Hezekiah's huge, incredible tunnel—cut through 1750 feet of solid rock—carried water from the Virgin's Fountain to the residents. Caesar's theater and amphitheater adorned the city. An immense, eye-catching bridge spanned the "Valley of Cheesemongers," connecting the eastern and western hills of Jerusalem. Buildings associated with government and religion stood out prominently all over the city. And at night, the illumination of the magnificent temple compound was breathtaking.[91]

Jerusalem was Jesus' destination, and he knew that what he would find there would be anything but peace.

The King's Arrival

Jesus, God's chosen King, "headed straight for Jerusalem" (Luke 19:28).

- *Just outside the city, what did Jesus say to two of his disciples (vv. 29–31)?*

- *What did the disciples discover as they carried out Jesus' instructions (vv. 32–34)?*

- *Read verses 35–40 and describe the welcome Jesus received as he made his entrance into the great city.*

- *While most people were rejoicing, what did Jesus do and say when he saw Jerusalem (vv. 41–44)?*

While Jesus knew his end was coming, he wept over the coming destruction of the great city he now entered. The city's political and religious leaders and many of its citizens and visitors had no clue that the Prince of Peace was entering their domain. And they would soon reject him and kill him, all the while claiming they were doing what was good and right to maintain peace in their fair city.

A House Cleaning

- *After entering the city, Jesus went to the "temple area and forcibly threw out all the merchants from their stalls" (v. 45). What did he tell them (v. 46)?*

 THE BACKSTORY

The Gospels record that Jesus purged the temple courts twice during his ministry: once near the start of his ministry (John 2:13–22) and then here toward the end of his ministry (Matthew 21:12–13; Mark 11:15–17; Luke 19:45–46). Why were these business dealings happening in the temple area anyway? Bible scholar John Martin answers:

> Money changing was done because only certain coinage was then accepted in the temple from those who bought animals for sacrifices. The religious leaders made money off the system of buying and selling animals for sacrifice (thus making the temple a den of robbers). Also they led the people into mere formalism. A pilgrim traveling to Jerusalem could go to the temple, buy an animal, and offer it as a sacrifice without ever having anything to do with the animal. This led to the impersonalization of the sacrificial system. The commercial system was apparently set up in the area of the temple which had been designated for devout Gentiles to pray and so was disrupting Israel's witness to the surrounding world.[92]

While the gentiles who were attempting to worship there must have delighted in Jesus' action, not everyone did.

- *Who despised Jesus' activity in the temple area, and what did they want to do to him? What made them hesitate before taking this action (Luke 19:47–48)?*

Putting the Critics in Their Place

Once in Jerusalem and having made his presence known in dramatic fashion by cleaning house at the temple, Jesus spent much of his time "teaching in the temple courts and sharing with the people the wonderful news of salvation" (Luke 20:1).

The Issue of Authority

- *On one of these teaching occasions, who confronted Jesus, and what was their demand (vv. 1–2)?*

- *Read the exchange between Jesus and his critics in verses 3–8 and explain why the men were unable to answer Jesus' question.*

⚡ DIGGING DEEPER

It was a common practice in Jesus' day to counter a question with another question. And Jesus did this because his questioners made an insincere demand. They had set a trap for him. They were using reason to put him on the horns of a dilemma. Their questions were designed to force Jesus to claim that his teaching and actions were justified by either God's authority or man's. If justified by God, then they could attack him as a false prophet. If by man, then they could claim that he was "a troublemaker bent on usurping Roman law and order."[93] A dilemma was designed to force a person to affirm at least one of two positions, neither of which, it was assumed, the person wanted to accept.[94] This was the trap Jesus' critics wanted him to fall into.

Jesus escaped their trap by posing to them a dilemma of his own: Did John the Baptizer "baptize because he had a commission from heaven or merely from men?" (v. 4). In other words, Jesus posed an authority dilemma that provided the same kind of quagmire that they had tried to put him in. His critics grasped this almost immediately. Discussing the problem together, they recognized that if they answered that John's ministry mandate came "from heaven," then why didn't they believe him and undergo his baptism of repentance? The other horn of the dilemma wasn't any better. If they claimed that John's ministry was "merely from men," then they would face the wrath of the people who believed that "John was a prophet of God." So rather than commit to one of the horns of the dilemma, Jesus' critics claimed ignorance. This gave Jesus an out from dealing with the dilemma they posed to him. Although he knew that his commission was from God, since his critics were just trying to trap him and not trying to learn from him, he felt no need to answer them.

⚘ EXPERIENCE GOD'S HEART

- *Has anyone ever challenged your right use of authority? If so, how did you handle it, and how did that work out for you?*

- *What can you learn from the way Jesus addressed challenges to his authority, not just in this situation, but from others we have encountered in Luke's Gospel (e.g., 5:20–25; 6:1–10; 7:37–50; 11:14–20)?*

A Judgment Warning

When Jesus continued with his teaching of the people, he used another parable.

- *Describe the behavior of the tenants in the story and the reasoning behind their actions (20:9–16).*

- *How did Jesus' audience respond to the story (v. 16)?*

- *What did Jesus explain about the story's meaning? Why did this offend the high priests, and what did they want to do to Jesus as a result (vv. 17–19)?*

- *Look up the passages that follow. What added insight do they provide for Jesus' interpretive comment about the cornerstone?*

    Psalm 118:22–23

    Isaiah 8:13–15

    Isaiah 28:16–17

- *Given all of this, why do you think the religious leaders saw Jesus' teaching here as especially directed at them?*

A Question of Taxes

While Jesus was teaching, the religious leaders sent "spies" to Jesus. They "pretended to be honest seekers," but what they really wanted was "an opportunity to entangle Jesus by his words" (Luke 20:20).

- *What was the plan of the spies (v. 20)?*

- *After flattering Jesus (v. 21), what did they ask him (v. 22)?*

- *Read verses 23–26. Describe how Jesus handled their ploy and how it worked out for the spies.*

 DIGGING DEEPER

Once again, Jesus' critics tried to catch him on the horns of a dilemma, this time using taxes as the foil. The dilemma was a difficult one, as Christian philosopher Douglas Groothuis explains:

> If he sided with the Pharisees, he might be
> seen as an insurrectionist and a dangerous
> element (as were the Zealots, Jews who
> defended violent revolution against the
> state). If Jesus affirmed paying taxes, he

would be viewed as selling out to a secular
and ungodly power instead of honoring
Israel's God. He would be denounced
as disloyal. This was not a "win-win"
situation.[95]

Jesus found a brilliant way to escape from between the horns of the dilemma. Rather than affirm either bad option, "Jesus gives a place to the rule of Caesar under God without making Caesar God. Caesar's portrait on the coin (a bust of Tiberius) had an inscription ascribing deity to the emperor. When he differentiates Caesar from God, he strips Caesar of his supposed deity."[96] Jesus' answer, then, showed that neither horn of the dilemma belonged to him. He was neither a disloyal Jew nor an insurrectionist. He recognized the temporal governing authority but put it where it belongs—under the cosmic authority of the Lord of lords and King of kings (cf. John 19:10–11). For what doesn't ultimately belong to God (see Psalm 24)?

The Truth about Resurrection

Still seeking a way to trap Jesus, "Some of the Sadducees (a religious group that denies there is a resurrection of the dead) came to ask Jesus this question" (Luke 20:27).

- *Lay out the situation these Sadducees presented and then the dilemma they put to Jesus to solve (vv. 28–33).*

- *Can you specify what the horns of the dilemma were? If so, do that below.*

- *Once again, Jesus escaped from the horns of the dilemma. First, he challenged the Sadducees' poor theology of marriage. What did he say that refuted their view (vv. 34–36)?*

- *Next Jesus did something subtle and profound. The Sadducees only accepted the Pentateuch (the first five books of the Bible) as the authoritative Word of God. And they rejected what most other Jews believed, which was the general resurrection of the dead before the ultimate judgment of God (Acts 4:1–2; 23:7–8; cf. John 11:23–25; Isaiah 26:19; Daniel 12:2). One of the most foundational passages of the Sadducees was Exodus 3:6. Look up that passage and write it out below.*

- *Now return to Luke 20:38. What did Jesus say in light of the passage from Exodus?*

The Exodus passage does not say "I *was* the God of…" Rather, it says "I *am* the God of…" Jesus argued from a verb tense that God *is* the God of the living, not of the dead. He still is the God of Abraham, Isaac, and Jacob. How can that be? Because the Jewish fathers were still alive! Their bodies were in the ground, but there is still something about them that lives on. Jesus had dramatically demonstrated this when Moses and Elijah appeared with him and with some of his disciples as witnesses (Luke 9:28–35).

So the Sadducees, who rejected the resurrection, had to face their own dilemma. They were wrong about marriage (so they had to rethink that), and one of the biblical passages that they regarded as the most significant actually assumes life after death, something they had denied. What, now, were they going to do with that passage of Scripture and with the insight that Jesus brought from it?

The trappers became the trapped. The hunted One had caught them. This is why "the religious Sadducees never dared ask Jesus a question again" (Luke 20:40).

David and the Messiah

Jesus then took the opportunity to pose his own dilemma to the people listening to him.

- *What is the dilemma? See if you can write it out in your own words (vv. 41–44).*

Through posing this dilemma, Jesus reduced the position of the religious leaders to an absurdity while also attempting to open their blind eyes. He had already accepted the attribution of being the son of David (see Luke 18:35–41), and he had been raised by parents who were in David's ancestral line (see 1:26–27; 2:4). Even the angel Gabriel had told Mary, his mother, that Jesus would be enthroned "as King on the throne of his ancestor David" (1:32). Jesus had a Davidic identity and self-awareness.

The issue Jesus raised to the people was this: Is the Messiah from David's ancestral line merely a human son? Jesus then quoted from Psalm 110:1, a psalm of David, where David revealed that Yahweh is called the Messiah, the one who would come from David, "Lord." So Jesus asked, if David calls the Messiah his Lord, how is this Messiah David's son? If the Messiah is merely a human son, then he could not be the Lord. But if he is the Lord, he can't be merely a human son. The options the dilemma gives lead to absurdities: (1) the Messiah being *only* human yet divine also; or (2) the Messiah being *only* divine and yet human also. Each option is illogical, irrational, contradictory. A being cannot be only human yet not human at all or only not human yet human. We might as well be talking about square circles, which makes no sense either.

So what's the answer? What's the escape from the dilemma? Jesus did not provide it, but from his own teaching and ministry, he left the opportunity open for his listeners to provide it: The Messiah is both human *and* divine, both man *and* God, both David's son *and* God's Son; he is not merely human or merely divine but both human and divine at the same time.[97]

- *What do you think of the subtly of Jesus' reasoning abilities and knowledge of Scripture?*

Religious Pretensions

Jesus' dealings with his critics led him to warn his followers and other listeners about the pretensions of the religious leaders of his day.

- *What did Jesus say the religious leaders typically did (Luke 20:45–47)?*

- *What did Jesus say would eventually happen to them (v. 47)?*

- *Imagine one of the religious leaders hearing Jesus' indictment. How might that person have reacted to what he heard? How do you think Jesus hoped such people would react?*

Surplus vs. Sacrifice

Jesus witnessed a contrast when he saw people coming into the temple courts to make their offerings.

- *What did Jesus notice (21:1–2)?*

- *What action did Jesus commend and why (vv. 3–4)?*

 SHARE GOD'S HEART

- *Do you ever give sacrificially? If so, tell of one occasion. If not, why?*

- *What and to whom can you give that would not come from your surplus but would count as a sacrificial gift? Make plans for that to happen soon, perhaps in the next thirty days.*

Signs of the End of the Age

Some of Jesus' disciples commented to him about "the beauty of the temple" (21:5). And it was an incredible sight. The temple grounds were twenty-six acres.[98] The temple and its adjoining structures were built of "white stone blocks," and "crowning the [temple's] roof were golden spikes to prevent birds perching or nesting on it." Some of the walls in the temple complex were adorned with "geometric patterns and flowers."[99]

> The temple compound was constructed atop a mount which rose abruptly from deep valleys and towered over streets, houses, and businesses. It dominated the city—physically and spiritually. Impressive, intimidating walls surrounded this symmetrically proportioned one-thousand-square-foot structure. Terrace upon terrace thrust the temple skyward...On a clear day, the rays of the sun reflected off the pinnacle of this structure. The very appearance of the temple communicated the presence of the omnipotent, majestic God.[100]

What wasn't to like? The temple compound was an incredible architectural achievement.

- *What did Jesus say would happen to the temple (v. 6)?*

- *What questions did this dire prediction provoke from Jesus' disciples (v. 7)?*

- *Jesus' response was a combination of what will happen, how his followers should respond to it all, and why. On your computer or a piece of paper, create a chart with two columns. On top of the lefthand column, put the heading "What's Coming." On the top of the righthand column, place the heading "What Disciples Should Do and Why." Then read verses 8–36 and fill in the chart with the appropriate information.*

🕐 DIGGING DEEPER

Jesus' prediction about the destruction of Jerusalem and its temple came to pass in AD 70. In the year 66, multiple disputes led to a Jewish insurrection that generated violent confrontations with Rome. In his work *The Jewish War*, the ancient historian Josephus goes into great detail about the events that led up to the conflict, how the rebellion then unfolded, and how Rome and its military and political leaders responded. He also writes about the Jewish religious leaders and the various ways they either helped the rebels or sided with Rome against them. His description of the eventual siege of the city of Jerusalem, the famine and desperation that ensued within the city walls, and the various breaches of the walls, the killing, the destruction of property, and the complete wreckage of the temple is horrifying reading. He tells about one desperate mother who killed her baby son, roasted him, and ate part of him just to survive.[101] Josephus claimed that more than a million people lost their lives in the battles for Jerusalem and that the Romans took about ninety-seven thousand people captive during the entire war, which lasted from 66 to 73.[102]

In Jesus' prediction about this desolation, he warned that when people saw armies surrounding Jerusalem, those living in Judea should "flee to the mountains," those living inside Jerusalem should leave it and flee, and those living outside of the city should not enter it hoping to find refuge (Luke 21:20–21). Those who knew of and believed Jesus' prediction followed his counsel even before war broke out in 66. Many Christians left the area and went to Pella, which was in the province of Perea, a mostly gentile area.[103] Other Christians traveled east of the Jordan River and the Dead Sea and even into Egypt. Many also went into Asia (modern-day Turkey).[104]

Anyone who stayed in Judea, especially in Jerusalem, lost their life either through death, imprisonment, or forced servitude.

- *Given the accuracy of Jesus' prediction concerning the destruction of Jerusalem and its temple, what does that tell you about how much you can count on the rest of what he predicted coming true?*

- *Are you preparing yourself for the end of days—a period that began in the first century? Reread what Jesus said about how we should live in this period of history. What are you ready for? What else do you need to prepare for?*

Talking It Out

1. While Jesus recognized the role of temporal governing authority and its rights, he also put it where it belonged; its authority was derived from the God who created the universe and rules over it. Every Jew understood that no human authority stood independent from the God of ultimate cosmic authority. How does this understanding help us in our dealings with government? What support does it afford us? What conflicts might it bring us?

2. Jesus was a brilliant thinker. He reasoned far better than his contemporaries, and he knew Scripture and its subtleties so well that he could stump the best exegetes of Judaism. To put it bluntly, Jesus could not be bested. But he used his abilities to teach the truth, "to achieve understanding or insight in his hearers."[105] His driving purpose was not to win arguments (though that happened) but to change minds and hearts. Reflect on Jesus' use of reason and Scripture, discuss it in your group, and consider how you can become Christlike in these ways.

LESSON 11

Passover and Betrayal

(22:1–23:25)

After Jesus silenced his critics, he continued to teach in the temple courts by day and spent his nights on the Mount of Olives (Luke 21:37). This mount is "a limestone ridge, rather more than a mile in length, running in general direction N and S and covering the whole eastern side of the city of Jerusalem." It has at least three "independent summits or natural elevations." [106] If one wanted to get to Bethany from Jerusalem, one had to cross the Mount of Olives. The garden of Gethsemane was located here. When Jesus came down into Jerusalem and was heralded as king, he came down this mount—a mount that rose some 250 feet above Jerusalem.[107] And it was during his descent, when he could see the great city of Jerusalem lying before him, that Jesus cried over the city and lamented its coming destruction (19:41–44).

Centuries before, the prophet Ezekiel had a vision of the glory of the Lord leaving Jerusalem. As the glory of the Lord lifted away, it "went up from the city and stopped above the mountain to the east" (Ezekiel 11:23 NLT). This mountain was the Mount of Olives. But when Jesus entered Jerusalem *from* the Mount of Olives, the glory of God returned to the city. Emmanuel, God with us, was there in the person of Jesus Christ (Matthew 1:23). But even the very presence of God in the flesh would not be enough to win some people to embrace him. Instead, Jesus would face an underhanded betrayal and a horrible death. The way of life is costly, and Jesus' life shows this.

The Betrayer

Luke 22 opens with trouble simmering.

• *Who was still looking for a way to kill Jesus (22:1–2)?*

• *Who decided to betray Jesus and with the help of whom (vv. 3–5)?*

• *For what was the betrayer willing to do the deed (v. 5; cf. Matthew 26:14–15 and study note 'f' for verse 15)?*

• *All this occurred during the preparation time for what Jewish feast (Luke 22:1–2)? What is the purpose of this religious observance, and how does it relate to what was about to happen to Jesus? Be sure to consult study note 'b' and look up the Old Testament passages listed there to more fully inform your answer.*

The Last Supper

- *Read Luke 22:7–13 and explain what happened when Jesus sent Peter and John to prepare for the Passover. Also consult study notes 'd' and 'e' for additional insights.*

- *Now in the upper room with "all the apostles"—in other words, the closest twelve disciples, which included Judas Iscariot, the one who would betray Jesus—the Lord shared their final meal together (v. 14). What did Jesus tell them about how important it was to him to share this meal with them (vv. 15–16)?*

- *With what words did Jesus present the wine and bread to his followers (vv. 17–22)?*

- *Which statement of Jesus' was most upsetting to the apostles (v. 23; cf. v. 21)? What does this reveal about the knowledge that eleven of the disciples had about the plot to betray Jesus?*

- *Superiority became another topic of discussion during the last supper. What brought this up, and what did Jesus have to say about it (vv. 24–30)?*

- *After the meal, Jesus singled out Peter. What did he tell this follower (vv. 31–32)?*

- *This provoked an exchange between Peter and Jesus. Read verses 33–34 and summarize how Jesus predicted the testing of Peter's faith in him.*

- *As Jesus and his disciples prepared to leave the upper room, Jesus gave them final instructions. What were they (vv. 35–38)?*

- *Reflect over this Passover meal. Would you say that the Twelve grasped what Jesus told them about what was soon to occur and its implications? Explain your answer.*

DIGGING DEEPER

Luke records that before Jesus began his ministry, Satan tried to entice Jesus away from initiating his mission (Luke 4:1–13). Satan's attempts failed. Now, toward the close of Jesus' ministry, Satan sought to end Jesus and abort the mission Jesus had left to his disciples, especially to the Twelve. This is not to say that Satan had been leaving Jesus alone until now, and Jesus certainly had not left Satan unopposed. Jesus had been casting out demons and even sending out his followers to do the same in his name. The demons even knew Jesus' true identity when they encountered him, and they feared him. Jesus also took on critic after critic and survived every attempt to trap him and stop him. Satan had been experiencing loss after loss. But with Judas, Satan secured a beachhead. Satan entered Judas and urged him to betray the man who had been his teacher, leader, equipper, friend, and confidant. Through Judas, Satan sought to destroy Jesus.

Moreover, Satan had also gone after Peter so he could use Peter to take down the rest of the Twelve. The metaphor of sifting Peter and the rest of the disciples "like wheat" (22:31) "implies violent shaking, in this case, to separate them from Jesus and to eliminate them from salvation. Satan in his arrogance sets out to bring the faithful crashing down (see Job 1:8–12; 2:3–7; Luke 8:12–15)." But Jesus, due to intercessory prayer, "can give Peter the ultimate assurance that his faith will not be eclipsed. He will lead the disciples in falling before he will turn around and lead them in their rising." [108]

In Jesus, Satan met more than his match. He met his superior in every way. Even at the end of Jesus' earthly life, Satan would not get his way—no matter how devious his methods and diabolical his ends.

EXPERIENCE GOD'S HEART

Jesus, God's own Son, revealed that the leadership model he favored was that of a servant—one who looks out for others more than oneself (Luke 22:25–27).

- *Do you have a servant's heart? If so, what would others point to as evidence of that interior orientation of your life?*

- *If you think of yourself and your needs more than you think of others, why is this so? What can you do to begin to live and lead more other-oriented than self-oriented?*

Gethsemane

After they left the upper room, Jesus led his disciples to the Mount of Olives (v. 39). Luke doesn't say where on the mount they went, but other Gospel writers do. It was to a garden grove known as Gethsemane, the place where Jesus liked to go for prayer (Matthew 26:36; Mark 14:32). "Jesus knew Gethsemane well. He knew that the road to Jericho was easily and quickly accessible from the place where He knelt to pray. He had friends in Jericho. Also close by was the route He frequently had traveled to Bethany. Probably His best friends in the world were there."[109] Gethsemane means "oil press." It was an "olive grove at the foot of the Mount of Olives."[110]

- *Once there, what did Jesus ask his disciples to do (Luke 22:40)?*

- *What, then, did Jesus do, and what was the experience like for him (vv. 41–44)?*

- *When he returned to his followers, what did Jesus find them doing, and what did he tell them (vv. 45–46)?*

⊘ DIGGING DEEPER

Jesus' prayer session was not serene and peaceful. He "wrestled with his Father's will more than at any other time in his earthly life...He had repeatedly predicted his crucifixion and labored to prepare his followers. Still, when such an excruciating death loomed imminent, he became overwhelmed, even terrified."[111] Bible scholar Curtis Mitchell brings this out in his discussion of this prayer session:

> Luke records Christ simply as kneeling;
> Matthew pictures Him as prostrate upon
> the ground, and Mark says He repeatedly
> fell to the ground! Putting all three
> [accounts] together, Christ probably first fell
> to His knees and as the agony intensified,

He literally prostrated Himself. Then, in the
height of the prayer struggle, He was in
such torment of soul that he was literally
writhing in anguish upon the ground…

The language of this prayer pictures
a small child crying out in desperation to
His daddy in the most intimate language
possible![112]

It's little wonder that during his prayer time, Jesus' agony was
so great that "his sweat became drops of blood, dripping onto the
ground" (Luke 22:44).

- *Have you ever struggled with God in prayer? What was
  that like? What was the outcome?*

Betrayal and Arrest

Immediately began the chain of events that Jesus had long
predicted.

- *Who came out to seize and arrest Jesus? Who identified
  Jesus, and how did he do it (Luke 22:47–48, 52)?*

In Jesus' day, a kiss between men was not unusual. "One normally greeted a teacher or rabbi with a kiss on the hand or on the
cheek if one considered oneself to be an equal"[113] (see Luke 7:45;
Acts 20:37; 1 Thessalonians 5:26). In the case of Judas, he turned
a greeting into an arrest identification, a sign of friendship and
respect into a betrayal.

- *Read Luke 22:49–51. How did Jesus' disciples react to Jesus' arrest, and what did Jesus do to deescalate the situation? Consult study note 'b' for verse 50 to glean more information about what happened.*

- *What did Jesus say to the authorities who came to arrest him (vv. 52–53)?*

- *What do Jesus' words suggest about the motives and method of the arresting authorities?*

- *Have you ever witnessed or learned about civil or religious authorities taking actions against a person or group that were comparable to what Jesus experienced? If so, describe the incident and how it affected you.*

Trials and Interrogation

Jesus' arrest was sanctioned by and largely carried out by Jewish religious authorities. John adds that they brought with them some Roman soldiers as well (John 18:3). But arresting Jesus was not enough to get him convicted and executed. The religious authorities had to find the necessary grounds for execution. That was what Jesus' trials and interrogations were supposed to achieve.

Annas

The arresting authorities first took Jesus to the "home of the high priest" (Luke 22:54). This man's name was Annas, and he had served as high priest from AD 6 to 15. When Jesus came before him (likely in the year 33[114]), Annas was still a powerful part of the aristocracy in Jerusalem. Five of his sons had been high priests, and the official high priest that Jesus would soon stand before, Caiaphas, was Annas's son-in-law. According to historian Paul Maier, "It was not only as a mark of respect to his authority, but possibly also in the nature of a preliminary, lower court hearing that Jesus was first brought before the patriarch Annas, who could still be called 'high priest,' much as ex-governors today are still called Governor So-and-so out of courtesy."[115]

- *Read John 18:19–24. What information do you think Annas was trying to get from Jesus? Did anyone produce any evidence that would count toward Jesus as a criminal?*

Annas's residence was likely in a palace in southwestern Jerusalem. Caiaphas also probably lived there, and a courtyard separated their spacious apartments.[116]

Around the time that Annas was interrogating Jesus, Peter, who had followed him there, stayed out in a nearby courtyard (Luke 22:54–55).

- *Read Luke 22:56–62. What accusations did the three bystanders make against Peter? How did Peter respond to each?*

- *Have you ever, in a crucial moment, denied the truth you knew? How did you feel afterward? How did that choice impact you in other ways?*

- *How was Jesus treated by some of his captors (vv. 63–65)?*

Caiaphas

- *What happened with Jesus at daybreak (vv. 66–71)?*

- *Matthew provides a fuller account of Jesus' trial and conviction in his Gospel. Read Matthew 26:57–68 and record below any details that Luke does not include in his more summarized version.*

- *Given all that you've read, what crime did the religious leaders finally charge Jesus with? Was this a civil charge or a religious one?*

Commenting on this verdict, Maier writes: "Jesus' claim to be Messiah was either true or false, and should have been examined in detail by Caiaphas."[117] Instead, the religious leaders showed a rush to judgment. Rather than seek the truth, they chose to push Jesus closer to death.

Pilate

- *Continuing his account, Luke says that the religious leaders "took Jesus to Pilate, the Roman governor" (Luke 23:1). What were the charges they presented to Pilate, and how did those allegations differ from what the religious leaders actually charged Jesus with (v. 2)?*

- *What was Pilate's initial conclusion after questioning Jesus himself (vv. 3–4)?*

- *What, then, did the religious leaders and the crowd of people charge Jesus with, and how did those allegations compare with the original charge (v. 5)?*

Herod Antipas

- *What led Pilate to send Jesus to the tetrarch Herod Antipas (vv. 6–7)?*

- *Describe what happened with Herod Antipas and how it influenced Herod's relationship with Pilate (vv. 8–12).*

 THE BACKSTORY

Luke doesn't tell us what the "long-standing feud" between Pilate and Herod Antipas was (v. 12), but Josephus and other accounts of the time give some insight into what led to their animosity. Before the Jesus incident, Pilate set up several golden shields in his Jerusalem headquarters (which was the palace that Herod the Great had built; Philo called it the "house of the governors"). These shields had no images on them, just an inscription of dedication to the Roman Emperor Tiberius. But the Jews, who were led by Herod Antipas and his brothers, protested against the shields, and Pilate refused to remove them. Herod Antipas formally protested Pilate's action to Tiberius. Tiberius then sent Pilate a stern letter in which he ordered Pilate to move the shields to a temple in Caesarea and warned him to uphold the religious and political customs of the Jews in Judea. Pilate, then, succumbed to the pressure and removed the shields.[118]

No doubt Pilate and Herod Antipas remained at odds with each other until the Jesus situation came along. Pilate knew that Herod wanted to have some time with Jesus, and when he sent Jesus over, Herod must have been pleased with the gesture of goodwill.

Pilate Again

- *Now back in Pilate's jurisdiction, whom did the Roman governor gather (vv. 13–14)?*

- *According to Pilate, what now was the charge against Jesus? Did Pilate think that Jesus was guilty of this charge, and what did he say that Herod Antipas had concluded (vv. 13–16)?*

- *Although civil authorities had declared Jesus to be an innocent man, what did Pilate suggest should be done to him (vv. 15–17)?*

- *An exchange ensued between the gathered crowd (which would have included the religious leaders) and Pilate. Read verses 18–25. What does the crowd demand, and how does Pilate respond?*

Did Pilate have to deliver Jesus over for crucifixion? Not at all. As Larry Overstreet states at the end of his scholarly essay "Roman Law and the Trial of Christ":

When Pilate delivered Christ to be crucified he demonstrated "all the cowardice of the judge who thus declines to act as the protector of the innocence," and the natural principles of equity which should have been allowed to an alien (although not required by Roman law) were denied.

What could Pilate have done instead of sending Christ to the cross? He could have displayed the fortitude to do what was morally and ethically right, and then relied on the emperor's sense of justice if the matter had been brought before him. The proconsul of Achaia, Gallio by name, did this very thing when the Apostle Paul was brought before him (Acts 18:12–17); he refused to hear the case and literally drove the complainers from his presence. Pilate could have done this, but instead he chose to follow what he thought was the politically expedient route and sent Christ to the cross.[119]

❤ SHARE GOD'S HEART

Often Christians think that Christlikeness equals niceness, that being like Christ means not creating waves, making the people around them feel safe, secure, and unchallenged. Was that how Jesus lived? Did he go to the cross because he was so nice, so unoffensive, so placid, so comfortable to hear and be around? Did his ministry always bring smiles and shouts of joy from others? Or was he sometimes offensive and challenging? Did he threaten the status quo and the religious and political elite? Did he go against cultural norms?

The best way to share God's heart is to be more and more like his Son in all we say and do. Will that always be well received? No.

Will it sometimes offend others? Yes. Christians will be opposed as their Lord was opposed. To identify with him and to spread the truth about him and why he came will foster opposition at times. Perhaps that's one way of knowing how well we are standing up for him—namely, that we sometimes face challenges for doing that. That should not lead us to cower but to stand with courage and conviction.

- *How are you sharing God's heart about Jesus Christ in a situation that may oppose him? What does your witness for him look like?*

- *Have you received any opposition, any challenges to your witness for Christ? If not, why do you think this is so? If you have, what shape have those challenges taken and how effectively are you dealing with them?*

Talking It Out

1. Jesus habitually went to the Mount of Olives to pray. Do you have a place in which you like to pray? If so, where? How did you come to choose this place? When you can't go there, where else do you find conducive for prayer?

2. Jesus' trials and the miscarriage of justice that followed are not new. Injustice had been a problem in human history before Jesus arrived to stand before Pilate, and it has been since. What led to Jesus being so hated, so despised, that some people sought his death? Reflect on Luke's account of Jesus' ministry to pull together the various strands that provide an answer to this question.

3. Up to this point in Luke's Gospel, it appears that Satan had gotten his way, that his plan had succeeded. Jesus was headed to the cross, an innocent man but condemned to death. And Peter's loyalty ended in three denials that disassociated him from Jesus. The scene was bleak. Have you ever experienced a dark time in your life—a time that seemed desperate and hopeless? Tell what happened, how you felt, and what you learned from it.

LESSON 12

Death and Beyond

(23:26–24:53)

Jesus had been sentenced.

His execution was assured.

He was going to The Skull (Luke 23:33) to be crucified. In Aramaic, this place was known as *Golgotha* (John 19:17), and it was outside of Jerusalem's outer walls. The holy city had rejected the holiest One of all, with religious and civic leaders participating in the events that led to his execution.

Crucifixion had a long history. Created in the ancient Near East, it had been used by the Persian ruler Darius I to execute three thousand political enemies in Babylon in 519 BC. This was the same king who supported and helped finance the restoration of the Jerusalem temple and saw it to its completion in 516–515 BC (Haggai 1:1; Zechariah 1:1; Ezra 6:1–15).[120] The Romans learned about crucifixion from their enemies, the Carthaginians, who used it to punish and execute "their admirals for losing sea battles to Rome."[121]

When the Romans began using crucifixion, the response to it was horror. Cicero, the great Roman statesman and lawyer, called it "the cruelest and most hideous punishment" possible.[122] It was such an awful way to die that the Romans reserved the punishment for "slaves, pirates, and those political or religious rebels who had to suffer an exemplary death."[123] Jesus, of course, did not fit into any of these categories. Even Pilate and Herod Antipas thought him innocent, having done nothing to deserve death. And yet, Jesus had been sentenced to die by crucifixion. Why? Apparently, the rationale they settled on was political subversion. Nailed on the head of Jesus' cross was an inscription: "This man is the king of all the Jews" (Luke 23:37–38). When Pilate called out to the people, "Shall I nail your king to a cross?" the high priests yelled back, "We have no other king but Caesar!" (John 19:15). So Pilate insisted that Jesus' kingship be the official and publicly displayed charge for his execution (vv. 19–22). While no evidence had been presented that Jesus was an enemy of the Roman state—a man claiming to be a political king rivaling and subverting Caesar (18:33–37)—he was executed as if he were such an enemy.

Death Has Its Day

Luke leaves out the brutal flogging and mocking Jesus received before Roman guards led him to the execution site (see Matthew 27:26–31). By the time Jesus' Roman captors had finished with his pre-crucifixion beating, Jesus had already lost blood and a good deal of his strength.

The Way to the Skull

It was a Roman custom for the person condemned to be crucified to carry one of the crossbeams to which he would be nailed.[124] The prisoner would thereby demonstrate to those watching that he had finally submitted to Rome's rule.[125]

- *As Jesus was carrying his crossbeam through the streets of Jerusalem, whom did the soldiers meet, and what did they force him to do (Luke 23:26)?*

- *Who was following Jesus, and what did Jesus say to them (vv. 27–31)?*

Commenting on Jesus' words to these women, David Garland writes:

> Jesus does not offer comfort to the women who openly bemoan his fate but heightens their pain with a prophetic warning about the fall of Jerusalem. What is now happening to him has been determined by God (9:31; 18:31; 22:22, 37; 24:25–26; 24:44, 46; Acts 2:23; 3:18; 4:25–28; 13:27–29). He goes to the cross knowingly and obediently, faithful to the mission given him according to God's redemptive will ([Luke] 9:22; 13:33; 17:25; 24:7, 26). He is not the one to be pitied; they are…
>
> …Just as he wept over the city on his entrance (19:41–44), so now on his exit he expresses grief over the coming devastation that will consume the innocent.[126]

 EXPERIENCE GOD'S HEART

Grief, unfortunately, is part of life in our fallen, broken world. Jesus experienced it, and so did the people who mourned over his impending death.

- *Have you experienced a similar degree of sadness and loss? Over what or whom did you grieve?*

- *Did you recover from this experience? If so, how?*

- *Great loss creates wounds that may never completely heal, at least on this side of heaven. But they can work to change us for the good—for example, to soften us toward the hurt others experience. What have you learned through your time of grief that has helped you?*

Crucifixion

- *Now at the crucifixion site, who else was condemned along with Jesus, and where was his cross placed in relation to them (Luke 23:32–33)?*

In the case of these condemned men, spikes were used to nail them to their crosses. Paintings typically show spikes driven through the palms of the hands of Jesus, but that would not have borne Jesus' weight. In the summer of 1968, archaeologists discovered the remains of a man who had been crucified in the first century. This condemned man's name was Yehohanan Ben-Hagakol. His wounds showed "that a nail had penetrated between the two bones of his lower forearm just above the wrist." Also, a "large, rusty iron spike, seven inches long" was discovered that "had been driven through both heel bones after first penetrating an acacia wood wedge or plaque that held the ankles firmly to the cross."[127] Along with forearms nailed to the horizontal beam and heels nailed to the vertical beam, the executed had a peg (or block) to sit on—a peg that had been pounded into the midsection of the cross. This small seat provided a little relief to the victim's agony.

Their crosses may have been quite tall if the Romans wanted the crucified to be seen from some distance away. Typically, however, the cross rose about seven feet from the ground. This made it possible for carnivorous animals to reach the hanging dead.[128]

- *What did Jesus keep saying as the Roman guards nailed him to his cross (v. 34)?*

- *What did the Roman executioners do during and following their nailing of Jesus to the cross (vv. 34, 36, 37–38)?*

- *How did the religious leaders treat Jesus as he hung on the cross (v. 35)?*

- *What did the other crucified men say to Jesus, and how did he respond (vv. 39–43)?*

- *What happened during Jesus' final moments on the cross (vv. 44–46; also check out study notes 'a' and 'b' for a better understanding of these verses)?*

🎬 THE BACKSTORY

In verses 44–46, Luke records three events of great significance. First, the darkness that occurred from about noon to 3:00 p.m. cosmically symbolized the reign of darkness that had begun when Jesus was betrayed and arrested (22:53). Evil was having its way.

Nevertheless, and this was the second event, the sudden tearing in two of the veil that separated the Holy Place from the rest of the temple "symbolized the fact that now, because of Jesus' death, people had freer access to God."[129] They no longer had to rely on priests as mediators or on any other aspect of the sacrificial system. Jesus as their priest and sacrifice supplied all they needed for their approach to God (Ephesians 2:11–18; Hebrews 7:26–27; 9:1–5, 12–15; 10:8–10). So the one whom evil meant to destroy through crucifixion—namely, Jesus—God worked through to bring about good for all humanity. Jesus' death gave us immediate access to God's life.

Finally, Luke tells us that Jesus chose when to yield his life to the Father. He gave up his life freely as an act of submission to his heavenly Father. Evil had tried to impose death upon him, but Jesus took that power away in his final moments (cf. John 10:14–15, 17–18).

On the surface, Jesus crucified looks like a victory for Satan and all he stands for. In reality, however, God turned the crucifixion of his Son into a death blow to Satan and an open road of access to everlasting life for all human beings who place their faith in Christ.

From the Cross to the Tomb

Next Luke tells us about the reactions of some of the people who witnessed Jesus' death on the cross.

- *Read Luke 23:47–56 and then describe what the people below did after Jesus breathed his last.*

    A Roman captain –

    The crowds –

    Those who knew Jesus (disciples), especially the women –

    Joseph, a member of the Jewish council –

 THE BACKSTORY

Where were the Twelve? We know from John's Gospel that John witnessed Jesus' crucifixion as did Mary, Jesus' mother (John 19:25–27). Also, we learn from Matthew that Judas had returned the blood money he had received as payment for his betrayal of Jesus, and then he committed suicide (Matthew 27:3–5). But what about the rest of the Twelve? Where were they when Jesus died? They had abandoned him. And they were in hiding within the confines of Jerusalem because they feared the Jewish leaders would come after them (Mark 16:13; Luke 24:33; John 20:19).

Women followers of Jesus were present at Jesus' crucifixion and at his burial. They also concerned themselves with completing the burial rites once the Sabbath day had come to an end (Luke 23:49, 55–56).

Also, an apparent witness of Jesus' crucifixion was a secret disciple, a Jewish council member named Joseph (vv. 50–54). With the help of another secret disciple, a Pharisee named Nicodemus (John 19:39–42; cf. 3:1), Joseph buried Jesus in an unused tomb that he owned (Matthew 27:59–60).

So the ones who cared for Jesus' body after his death were disciples, but none of them were among the Twelve—Jesus' closest disciples. And those present gave Jesus a burial that was uncommon for those who had been crucified. Normally the Romans refused burial to executed criminals. "Victims of crucifixion remained on their crosses as a matter of course, left to carrion birds as a continuing deterrent against crimes against the state." In rare cases, "the crucified were removed and given to their relatives for burial."[130] Of course, Joseph was not a relative, and yet Pilate turned Jesus' body over to him anyway (Luke 23:52).

Moreover, even when Jews provided executed criminals with a burial, they typically put the deceased into "shallow dirt graves in a plot reserved for that purpose."[131] They were not allowed to bury dead criminals in their family tombs (1 Kings 13:21–22; Jeremiah 26:23). Joseph, however, treated Jesus' body much differently. He followed, as much as he could with the little time he had, the typical burial customs of first-century Jews.

> When death occurred the eyes of the
> deceased were closed, the mouth bound
> up, the corpse washed…and anointed…
> The warm climate dictated a speedy burial,

with the use of spices necessary to counter the stench of decomposition. For the same reason the body might be laid on sand or salt. The deceased were buried in their own clothes or in specially prepared wraps... When the body was in place, the tomb was closed off by a large rock..., held in place by a smaller stone.[132]

It looked as if all were lost, that Jesus and his way had come to a horrific and definitive end. Even the women who had watched Jesus die and witnessed his burial planned to return to the tomb after the Sabbath to finish anointing Jesus' lifeless body with "fragrant spices and ointments" (Luke 23:56). No one expected him to rise from the dead.

Resurrection Victory

On Sunday morning, everything changed!

The Empty Tomb

• *Who arrived at Jesus' tomb and why (Luke 24:1, 10)?*

• *What did they find when they arrived, and what news did they receive from the men who appeared (vv. 2–7)?*

- *How did the women respond to the angelic messengers (vv. 8–9)?*

- *How did the other disciples react to the women's testimony (vv. 11–12)?*

- *Did Peter yet grasp what had happened (v. 12)?*

🕑 DIGGING DEEPER

Recall that the disciples had never comprehended Jesus' prophetic words about his resurrection (Luke 18:32–34; cf. Mark 9:9–10; John 2:18–22; 11:23–26). While they, like most other Jews, believed in a general resurrection of all the dead just before God's final judgment, the notion of the Messiah rising from the dead just did not compute.[133] So at this point in Luke's narrative, he's reporting that Jesus' disciples still didn't understand why Jesus' tomb was empty and what the angelic messengers meant about Jesus rising from the dead "on the third day" (Luke 24:7).

Also, the fact that Luke and all the other Gospel writers report that the women were the first witnesses to the empty tomb and Jesus' resurrection is just one of many facts that show that these writers are recording actual, historical events and not fantasy (Matthew 28:1–10; Mark 16:1–11; Luke 24:1–10; John 20:1–2,

11–18). You see, in ancient Jewish society, women were not typically regarded as reliable witnesses. "In the courts the testimony of women bore very little weight. Where their evidence was acceptable, so also was that of a Gentile slave."[134] Josephus even said, "From women let no evidence be accepted because of the levity and temerity of their sex."[135] So if the resurrection accounts were legend or myth, it would have been much more acceptable for men to have first discovered the empty tomb and received the resurrection message from angels. The fact that women were the first witnesses is a strong indication that what the Gospel writers recorded is historical—it really happened. Summarizing this testimony and drawing out some of its implications, Christian philosopher William Lane Craig states:

> Given the relatively low status of women in Jewish society and their lack of qualification to serve as legal witnesses, the most plausible explanation, in light of the Gospels' conviction that the disciples were in Jerusalem over the Easter weekend, why women and not the male disciples are described as discoverers of the empty tomb is that the women were in fact the ones who made this discovery. Moreover, why would the Christian church humiliate its leaders by having them hiding in cowardice in Jerusalem, while the women boldly carry out their last devotions to Jesus' body, unless this were in fact true? Finally, the listing of the women's names weighs against their discovery being a legend, for these persons were known in early Christian fellowship and could not be easily associated with a false account.[136]

An Unforgettable Lesson

On the same day that the women reported to the disciples what they had seen and heard, "two of Jesus' disciples were walking from Jerusalem to Emmaus, a journey of about seventeen miles" (Luke 24:13).

- *What topic of conversation occupied their time as they were traveling together, and who joined them? Why didn't these disciples recognize their rabbi (vv. 14–16)?*

- *Read verses 17–27 and summarize the exchange between Jesus and these followers.*

- *Imagine you had been one of these individuals and received the lesson they did from Jesus (v. 27). What do you think it would have been like for you to hear Jesus explain the Scriptures to you? How might it change your life?*

- *What happened when Jesus began to leave them (vv. 28–32)?*

• *What did these disciples do after Jesus disappeared (vv. 33–35)?*

Proof of Resurrection Life

To the Eleven, the two disciples who had been on the road to Emmaus, and perhaps other disciples in the Jerusalem place of hiding, Jesus suddenly appeared (v. 36).

• *Read verses 36–46. What does Jesus tell his disciples to convince them they do not need to be afraid? How does he demonstrate to them that he has actually risen physically from the dead?*

• *Jesus provided evidence for his resurrection reality. If you were asked to supply evidence that Jesus rose from the dead, what proof would you give?*

Remembrance and Mission

• *Jesus then gave his disciples a mission to fulfill. What was it (vv. 47–49)?*

 THE EXTRA MILE

While Luke does not record further appearances of the resurrected Jesus, a study of the other New Testament books, especially the other three Gospels, tells us about additional times Jesus appeared before he ascended into heaven.

- *Look up the passages in the chart below and record under the appropriate column whom Jesus appeared to, where the appearance occurred, and what he did to demonstrate his resurrection reality. The passages are listed in a suggested chronology of Jesus' appearances, and the Lukan appearances are not included. From what Scripture tells us, Jesus demonstrated he was alive by appearing bodily to more than five hundred people over a forty-day period on at least eleven occasions in a variety of circumstances.*

Passages	People Appeared To	Places of Appearance	Evidence of Jesus' Resurrection
John 20:11–18			
Matthew 28:9–10			
John 20:19–24			
John 21:1–23			
Matthew 28:16–20			
1 Corinthians 15:6			
1 Corinthians 15:7			
Acts 1:2–11			

♥ SHARE GOD'S HEART

Ever since Jesus gave his first disciples the mission to "go into all the nations and preach repentance and forgiveness of sin" (Luke 24:47), his followers have continued to take up the mantle of that mission. Some have become missionaries, others church planters, still others pastors and teachers. Over the centuries, Christians have learned that this mission can be carried out in whatever vocation they are in and while they are with anyone. All of us are Jesus' "witnesses" (v. 48). We are not among those who walked with Jesus in the first century, but we still walk with him in the power and light of the Spirit he sent. So we can tell others about how his resurrection life has and is transforming us, how he continues to bring people to him to enjoy and live out a life that is richer, deeper, and more satisfying than any life one tries to live apart from him. We can and should witness to Jesus' ongoing reality in our lives.

- *Consider how and to whom you can be a witness too. Pray that God will help prepare you and show Jesus through you. Then go and be yourself in Christ by the power of his Spirit. Be the conduit Christ desires, the witness of new life in him.*

Ascension

Luke closes his Gospel with another event that underscores the victory that Jesus has achieved by his death and resurrection. By his death, Jesus provided the once-for-all sacrifice sinful people (Jew and gentile) need to receive forgiveness and everlasting life from God. By his resurrection, Jesus defeated death so that all who believe in him will forever live beyond the grave (John 11:25–26; 1 Corinthians 15). Now Luke records Jesus' bodily reception into heaven—indicating that the Son's earthly mission was complete. What he had come to do had been accomplished. The next part of the divine mission will be carried out by Spirit-empowered and Spirit-gifted disciples.

- *Where did the resurrected Jesus take his disciples, and what happened there (Luke 24:50–52)?*

- *Where did the disciples go after Jesus ascended into heaven, and what did they do (vv. 52–53)?*

- *How did the disciples' demeanor differ from what it had been before they realized that Jesus had risen from the dead (see 24:2–4, 11–12, 17–18, 19, 24, 36–38, 41)?*

- *What do you think they now understood that they had not understood before?*

Not the End

Luke's Gospel ends with Jesus' ascension into heaven and the disciples in Jerusalem praising and worshiping God. Luke's book of Acts tells how the disciples were changed even more when they were "clothed with the mighty power of heaven" while still in Jerusalem. And then he provides us with the first history we have of the early church.

Two thousand years have passed since then, and the telling about Jesus, his teaching, his miracles, his death, his resurrection, and his ascension has continued on and reached worldwide. Lives are still changed because of this good news, and they will be until the one who bodily ascended into heaven returns bodily. But Jesus' second coming will be far different from his first. That, however, is for other books of Scripture to teach more fully.

For now, perhaps the best way to close our study of Luke is with the words of Brian Simmons, the translator of The Passion Translation:

> The one who walked with his friends on
> the way to Emmaus wants to walk with us.
> May we never walk in sadness or unbelief,
> for Jesus has risen from the grave and lives
> victorious as the living God in resurrection
> life! May you pause here and rejoice,
> believing that Jesus is the Christ, the Son
> of the living God and the only one who will
> bring us to the Father. Trust in him alone
> to save you, and you will spend eternity
> with him.[137]

Talking It Out

1. Jesus' crucifixion is the ultimate example of how God can bring good out of even the most horrendous evils. Discuss other examples, either from Scripture or elsewhere, that show God's ability to overcome evil by bringing good out of it. How might these examples give you confidence and hope in God that he can do this through your life's trials and hurts?

2. Reflect over all you have learned in your study of the Gospel of Luke. What life lessons stand out to you and why?

3. What did you study that you would like to dig into more? To get started, you may want to look through the sources cited in this study guide's endnotes. They can take you deeper into the topics covered in this guide.

Endnotes

1. Brian Simmons et al., "A Note to Readers," *The Passion Translation: The New Testament with Psalms, Proverbs, and Song of Songs* (Savage, MN: BroadStreet Publishing Group, 2020), ix.

2   See Luke's prologue in 1:1–4.

3   Brian Simmons, "Luke: Introduction: About Luke," *The Passion Translation: New Testament with Psalms, Proverbs, and Song of Songs* (Savage, MN: BroadStreet Publishing Group, 2020), 145–46.

4   William Steuart McBirnie, *The Search for the Twelve Apostles* (Wheaton, IL: Tyndale House, 1973), 268.

5   Joseph Fitzmyer, as quoted by McBirnie, *The Search for the Twelve Apostles*, 270.

6   Leon Morris, *Luke: An Introduction and Commentary*, Tyndale New Testament Commentaries (Downers Grove, IL: InterVarsity Press, 1988), 33.

7   Walter L. Liefeld, "Luke," *The Expositor's Bible Commentary* series vol. 8, gen. ed. Frank E. Gaebelein (Grand Rapids, MI: Zondervan, 1984), 802.

8   William Ramsay, as quoted by Morris, *Luke*, 41 and 41–42n69.

9   Simmons, "Luke: Introduction: Author and Audience," *The Passion Translation*, 147.

10 Richard L. Niswonger, *New Testament History* (Grand Rapids, MI: Zondervan, 1988), 267.

11 According to the Jewish historian and eyewitness Josephus, more than one million people in Jerusalem lost their lives. "Of those," he writes, "the largest number consisted of Jews by race, but not natives of Jerusalem; they had assembled from the whole country for the Feast of Unleavened Bread; and had suddenly been caught up in the war" (Josephus, *The Jewish War*, bk. 6, chap. 9, sec. 3). Some modern-day historians think Josephus's estimate is too high and put the number of people who died in the city closer to half a million or somewhat less. No matter the total number, the devastation upon the city and its temple was so great that it permanently altered the trajectory and practice of Judaism, and it shifted the heart of the new Christian movement from the center of Judaism to the larger gentile world.

12 For more on the dating of Luke's Gospel, see John A. T. Robinson, *Redating the New Testament* (Philadelphia, PA: Westminster Press, 1976), chap. 4; Donald Guthrie, *New Testament Introduction*, 4th ed. (Downers Grove, IL: InterVarsity Press, 1990), 125–31; Liefeld, "Luke," 807–9; Morris, *Luke*, 28–33.

13 John A. Martin, "Luke," *The Bible Knowledge Commentary: New Testament* (Wheaton, IL: Victor Books, 1983), 201.

14 Simmons, "Luke: Introduction: Major Themes," TPT, 147.

15 Robert H. Gundry, *A Survey of the New Testament*, rev. ed. (Grand Rapids, MI: Zondervan, 1981), 93.

16 Simmons, "Luke: Introduction," 147.

17 Morris, *Luke*, 56–57.

18 H. W. Hoehner, "Herodian Dynasty," *Dictionary of Jesus and the Gospels*, ed. Joel B. Green and Scot McKnight (Downers Grove, IL: InterVarsity Press, 1992), 318.

19 Hoehner, "Herodian Dynasty," *Dictionary of Jesus and the Gospels*, 319.

20 Hoehner, "Herodian Dynasty," *Dictionary of Jesus and the Gospels*, 320.

21 Paul L. Maier, *In the Fullness of Time: A Historian Looks at Christmas, Easter, and the Early Church* (San Francisco, CA: HarperSanFrancisco, 1991), 66.

22 Maier, *In the Fullness of Time*, 66–67.

23 Morris, *Luke*, 85.

24 See Luke 2:4–5, note 'e.'

25 Corey Piper, *500 Year Journey: From Babylon to Bethlehem* (New York: Morgan James, 2023), 78–79.

26 David E. Garland, *Luke*, Zondervan Exegetical Commentary on the New Testament series (Grand Rapids, MI: Zondervan, 2011), 117.

27 Piper, *500 Year Journey*, 82.

28 Harold W. Hoehner, *Chronological Aspects of the Life of Christ* (Grand Rapids, MI: Zondervan, 1977), 18–23. New Testament scholar F. F. Bruce also accepts this view of the census; see his *New Testament History* (New York: Doubleday & Co., 1969), 32.

29 Garland, *Luke*, 118.

30 Piper, *500 Year Journey*, 81.

31 C. Welton Gaddy, *Geography of the Soul* (Nashville, TN: Broadman & Holman, 1994), 30.

32 Gaddy, *Geography of the Soul*, 13.

33 Gaddy, *Geography of the Soul*, 14.

34 Gerald F. Hawthorne, *The Presence and the Power: The Significance of the Holy Spirit in the Life of Jesus* (Dallas, TX: Word, 1991), 99.

35 Hawthorne, *The Presence and the Power*, 102–3.

36 Hawthorne, *The Presence and the Power*, 26–27.

37 Niswonger, *New Testament History*, 129.

38 Niswonger, *New Testament History*, 129.

39 Hoehner, "Herodian Dynasty," *Dictionary of Jesus and the Gospels*, 322.

40 Martin, "Luke," 210.

41 Martin, "Luke," 212.

42 See Piper, *500 Year Journey*. Piper also explores other dates for Jesus' birth, but his primary goal is to arrive at the actual date of the Messiah's birth. He presents a fascinating, revealing, and compelling case for his

conclusion, which not only gives the year of Jesus' birth but even the month and the day.

43   For more on Jesus' possible birth date and age at the start of his ministry, see Piper, *500 Year Journey*, passim; Hoehner, *Chronological Aspects of the Life of Christ*, chap. 1–2; B. Witherington III, "Birth of Jesus"; and H. W. Hoehner, "Chronology" in *Dictionary of Jesus and the Gospels*, ed. Joel B. Green and Scot McKnight (Downers Grove, IL: InterVarsity Press, 1992), 60–74, 118–22.

44   Merrill F. Unger, *The New Unger's Bible Dictionary*, ed. R. K. Harrison (Chicago, IL: Moody Press, 1988), s.v. "Capernaum."

45   Morris, *Luke*, 129.

46   Morris, *Luke*, 135.

47   Here are some of the many helpful resources that provide evidence for the life, death, and resurrection of Jesus: Lee Strobel, *The Case for Jesus: A Journalist's Personal Investigation of the Evidence for Jesus* (Grand Rapids, MI: Zondervan, 1988); J. Warner Wallace, *Cold-Case Christianity: A Homicide Detective Investigates the Claims of the Gospels* (Colorado Springs, CO: David C. Cook, 2013); Gary R. Habermas, *The Verdict of History* (Eastbourne, Great Britain: Monarch, 1988); F. F. Bruce, *Jesus and Christian Origins Outside the New Testament* (Grand Rapids, MI: William B. Eerdmans, 1974); Michael J. Wilkins and J. P. Moreland, eds., *Jesus under Fire: Modern Scholarship Reinvents the Historical Jesus* (Grand Rapids, MI: Zondervan, 1995); Frank Morison, *Who Moved the Stone?*, reprint ed. (Grand Rapids, MI: Zondervan, 1971); and William Lane Craig, *Knowing the Truth about the Resurrection*, revised ed. (Ann Arbor, MI: Servant Books, 1988). Some excellent web sources are apologetics315.com, garyhabermas.com, and ngim.org.

48   Michael Griffiths, *The Example of Jesus* (Downers Grove, IL: InterVarsity Press, 1985), 22.

49   B. Gerhardsson, as quoted by Griffiths, *The Example of Jesus*, 23.

50   Martin, "Luke," 219.

51   To learn more about the spiritual disciplines and how to practice them, here are a few of the many available resources: Richard J. Foster, *Celebration of Discipline: The Path to Spiritual Growth*, revised ed. (San Francisco, CA: Harper & Row, 1988); Dallas Willard, *The Spirit of the Disciplines: Understanding How God Changes Lives* (San Francisco, CA: Harper & Row, 1988); William D. Watkins, *The Transforming Habits of a Growing Christian* (Minneapolis, MN: Bethany House, 2004); Donald S. Whitney, *Spiritual Disciplines for the Christian Life* (Colorado Springs, CO: NavPress, 1991); Klaus Issler, *Wasting Time with God: A Christian Spirituality of Friendship with God* (Downers Grove, IL: InterVarsity Press, 2001); Bruce Demarest, *Satisfy Your Soul: Restoring the Heart of Christian Spirituality* (Colorado Springs, CO: NavPress, 1999).

52   *The New International Dictionary of Biblical Archaeology*, ed. Edward M. Blaiklock and R. K. Harrison (Grand Rapids, MI: Zondervan, 1983), s.v. "Nain"; Martin, "Luke," 222.

53   Martin, "Luke," 223.

54   Garland, *Luke*, 347.

55   Charles Carlston, "Proverbs, Maxims, and the Historical Jesus," *Journal of Biblical Literature* 99 (1980), 95–96.

56   Richard N. Longenecker, *New Testament Social Ethics for Today* (Grand Rapids, MI: William B. Eerdmans, 1984), 73.

57   Morris, *Luke*, 169.

58   See Lawrence O. Richards, *Expository Dictionary of Bible Words* (Grand Rapids, MI: Zondervan, 1985), s.v. "Heart."

59   Morris, *Luke*, 173.

60   Resuscitation involves bringing a person back to life who will later die again. Resurrection, on the other hand, is bringing someone back to life who will never again experience physical death. There are also two different resurrections: one is from physical death to a forever life lived apart from God and in everlasting judgment; the other is from physical death to a forever life lived in joyous union with God and fully free from the devastating effects of sin. So far, Luke has told about resuscitations, not resurrections (7:11–15; 8:49–56).

61   Martin, "Luke," 243.

62   Watkins, *The Transforming Habits of a Growing Christian*, 87.

63   I. Howard Marshall, *The Gospel of Luke: A Commentary on the Greek Text*, The New International Greek Testament Commentary series (Grand Rapids, MI: William B. Eerdmans, 1978), 391.

64   Martin, "Luke," 231.

65   Garland, *Luke*, 416.

66   Garland, *Luke*, 436.

67   Watkins, *The Transforming Habits of a Growing Christian*, 250.

68   Watkins, *The Transforming Habits of a Growing Christian*, 251.

69   Watkins, *The Transforming Habits of a Growing Christian*, 252.

70   Richards, *Expository Dictionary of Bible Words*, s.v. "Glory."

71   Morris, *Luke*, 221.

72   Garland, *Luke*, 499.

73   Garland, *Luke*, 522.

74   Martin, "Luke," 239–40.

75   Maier, *In the Fullness of Time*, 146, 148.

76   Morris, *Luke*, 177.

77   Garland, *Luke*, 575

78   See note 'a' for Luke 15:12, TPT.

79   Henri Nouwen, *The Return of the Prodigal Son* (New York: Doubleday, 1992), 71.

80   Morris, *Luke*, 275.

81   Joel B. Green, *The Gospel of Luke*, The New International Commentary on the New Testament series (Grand Rapids, MI: William B. Eerdmans, 1997), 627.

82   Norman L. Geisler, *Systematic Theology, Volume Two* (Minneapolis, MN: Bethany House, 2003), 159.

83   The only reason Jesus could die is because he had a mortal human nature. He suffered death in his humanity, in his human body, not in his divine nature (Romans 8:3; Ephesians 2:15–16; Colossians 1:21–22; Hebrews 2:14; 10:19–20; 1 Peter 2:24). As the theologian and bishop Athanasius wrote in the fourth century: "The Word [the Son of God] perceived that corruption could not be got rid of otherwise than through death; yet He Himself, as the Word, being immortal and the Father's Son, was such as could not die. For this reason, therefore, He assumed a [human] body capable of death" (Athanasius, *On the Incarnation* [Crestwood, NY: St. Vladimir's Orthodox Theological Seminary, 1982], 35). Nowhere does the Bible say that God died on the cross. The Son of God, in his humanity, experienced death. Furthermore, neither the Father nor the Spirit suffered death because they were not incarnated.

84   Bruce, *New Testament History*, 133.

85   Garland, *Luke*, 763, 764.

86   Don Richardson, *Eternity in Their Hearts* (Ventura, CA: Regal Books, 1981), 7.

87   See Nahman Avigad, *Discovering Jerusalem* (Nashville, TN: Thomas Nelson, 1980), 23; *The Zondervan Pictorial Encyclopedia of the Bible*, gen. ed. Merrill C. Tenney (Grand Rapids, MI: Zondervan, 1976), vol. 3, s.v. "Jerusalem."

88   Gaddy, *Geography of the Soul*, 131–32.

89   Gaddy, *Geography of the Soul*, 132.

90   Robert Cornuke, *Temple* (Charlotte, NC: LifeBridge Books, 2014), 49.

91   Gaddy, *Geography of the Soul*, 132.

92   Martin, "Luke," 254.

93   Garland, *Luke*, 784.

94   For more on this type of argument, see Norman L. Geisler and Ronald M. Brooks, *Come, Let Us Reason: An Introduction to Logical Thinking* (Grand Rapids, MI: Baker Book House, 1990), 68–73.

95   Douglas Groothuis, *On Jesus* (Ontario, Canada: Wadsworth, 2003), 27.

96   Groothuis, *On Jesus*, 27.

97   Many people have claimed that Jesus as God and man at the same time is contradictory. For it seems the claim is that Jesus is both infinite and finite, eternal and temporal, immortal and mortal, divine and not divine at the same time. But that seems impossible. The answer takes a few hundred years in church history to fully articulate, but it comes to this:

Jesus has two natures: one is divine and the other is human. These natures co-exist in Jesus, remaining distinct but inseparable. In his divine nature, he is all that God is, such as infinite, eternal, immortal, immutable, and omniscient. While in his human nature, he is all that humanity is yet without sin: finite, temporal, mortal, mutable, and able to learn. A logical contradiction would result if Jesus were human and divine at the same time *and in the same way/manner.* But that is not what he is. Rather, he is divine in one nature and human in another nature. He is not divine *and* human in the *same* nature. This view of Jesus and his two distinct natures was eventually formulated in a creed that came out of the church council of Chalcedon in AD 451 (for the wording of the creed, see Henry Battenson and Chris Maunder, eds., *Documents of the Christian Church*, 3rd ed. [Oxford, England: Oxford University Press, 1999], 56–57). For more on this theological doctrine and its development, see Richard A. Norris Jr., ed., *The Christological Controversy*, Sources of Early Christian Thought series (Philadelphia, PA: Fortress Press, 1980); John D. Hannah, *Our Legacy: The History of Christian Doctrine* (Colorado Springs, CO: NavPress, 2001), chap. 4. Concerning the logical coherence of this doctrine, see Norman L. Geisler and William D. Watkins, "The Incarnation and Logic: Their Compatibility Defended," *Trinity Journal* (1985), vol. 6, 185–97; and Thomas V. Morris, *The Logic of God Incarnate* (Ithaca, NY: Cornell University Press, 1986).

98   F. F. Bruce, *Jesus and Paul: The Places They Knew* (Nashville, TN: Thomas Nelson, 1981), 61.

99   Alan Millard, *Treasures from Bible Times* (Tring, England: Lion Publishing, 1985), 169, 170.

100   Gaddy, *Geography of the Soul*, 156.

101   Josephus, *The Jewish War*, bk. 6, chap. 3, sec. 4.

102   Josephus, *The Jewish War*, bk. 6, chap. 9, sec. 3.

103   Eusebius, *Church History*, bk. 3, chap. 5, sec. 3.

104   See Bruce, *New Testament History*, 375–77.

105   Dallas Willard, "Jesus the Logician," in *The Best Christian Writing 2000*, ed. John Wilson (San Francisco, CA: HarperSanFrancisco, 2000), 265.

106   Unger, *The New Unger's Bible Dictionary*, s.v. "Olives, Mount of."

107   See Gaddy, *Geography of the Soul*, 168.

108   Garland, *Luke*, 869.

109   Gaddy, *Geography of the Soul*, 188.

110   Unger, *The New Unger's Bible Dictionary*, s.v. "Gethsemane."

111   Watkins, *The Transforming Habits of a Growing Christian*, 84.

112   Curtis C. Mitchell, *Praying Jesus' Way* (Old Tappan, NJ: Revell, 1977), 65.

113   Garland, *Luke*, 885.

114   Hoehner, *Chronological Aspects of the Life of Christ*, chaps. 4–5.

115   Maier, *In the Fullness of Time*, 137.

116   Maier, *In the Fullness of Time*, 137.

117 Maier, *In the Fullness of Time*, 139.

118 See Maier, *In the Fullness of Time*, 149; Hoehner, *Chronological Aspects of the Life of Christ*, 109–111.

119 R. Larry Overstreet, "Roman Law and the Trial of Christ," *Bibliotheca Sacra* (October–November 1978), 331.

120 *Nelson's New Illustrated Bible Dictionary*, gen. ed. Ronald F. Youngblood (Nashville, TN: Thomas Nelson, 1995), s.v. "Darius."

121 Maier, *In the Fullness of Time*, 164.

122 Cicero, as quoted by Maier, *In the Fullness of Time*, 164–65.

123 Maier, *In the Fullness of Time*, 165.

124 *The New International Dictionary of New Testament Theology*, ed. Colin Brown (Grand Rapids, MI: Zondervan, 1975), vol. 1, s.v. "Cross, Wood, Tree."

125 For more on this and its implications, see Michael P. Green, "The Meaning of Cross-Bearing," *Bibliotheca Sacra* 140 (April–June 1983), 117–33.

126 Garland, *Luke*, 918, 919.

127 Maier, *In the Fullness of Time*, 165.

128 Hans-Ruedi Weber, *The Cross: Tradition and Interpretation* (Grand Rapids, MI: William B. Eerdmans, 1975), 6.

129 Martin, "Luke," 263.

130 J. B. Green, "Burial of Jesus," in *Dictionary of Jesus and the Gospels*, 89.

131 See William Lane Craig, *Knowing the Truth about the Resurrection* (Ann Arbor, MI: Servant, 1981), 47–48.

132 Green, "Burial of Jesus," in *Dictionary of Jesus and the Gospels*, 89.

133 See Emil Schürer, *A History of the Jewish People in the Time of Jesus Christ* (Peabody, MA: Hendrickson, 1890), second division, vol. II, 179–81.

134 Mary J. Evans, *Woman in the Bible* (Downers Grove, IL: InterVarsity Press, 1983), 35.

135 Josephus, as quoted by Evans, *Woman in the Bible*, 35.

136 William Lane Craig, "Did Jesus Rise from the Dead?" in *Jesus under Fire*, eds. Wilkins and Moreland, 151.

137 Luke 24:53, note 'e,' TPT.